PARALLEL ARRAY PROCESSING

ELLIS HORWOOD SERIES IN ELECTRICAL AND ELECTRONIC ENGINEERING

Series Editors: PETER BRANDON, Emeritus Professor of Electrical and Electronic Engineering, University of Cambridge
P. R. ADBY, Department of Electronic and Electrical Engineering, University of London King's College

APPLIED CIRCUIT THEORY: Matrix and Computer Methods
P. R. ADBY, University of London King's College
BOND GRAPHS FOR MODELLING ENGINEERING SYSTEMS
ALAN BLUNDELL, Coventry (Lanchester) Polytechnic
NOISE IN ELECTRONIC DEVICES AND SYSTEMS
M. J. BUCKINGHAM, Royal Aircraft Establishment, Farnborough, Hampshire
DIGITAL AND MICROPROCESSOR ENGINEERING
S. J. CAHILL, Ulster Polytechnic
DIFFRACTION THEORY AND ANTENNAS
R. H. CLARKE and JOHN BROWN, Imperial College of Science and Technology, University of London
PARALLEL ARRAY PROCESSING
P. G. DUCKSBURY, Systems Designers Scientific, Gloucester
INTRODUCTION TO MICROCOMPUTER ENGINEERING
D. A. FRASER, *et al.,* Chelsea College, University of London
THEORY OF NON-LINEAR AND PARAMETRIC CIRCUITS
F. KOURIL and K. VRBA, University of Brno, Czechoslovakia
ELEMENTARY ELECTRIC POWER AND MACHINES
P. G. McLAREN, University Engineering Department, Cambridge
MICROWAVE PHASE MODULATORS
T. MORAWSKI and J. MODELSKI, Warsaw Technical University
CONTROL SYSTEMS WITH TIME DELAYS
A. W. OLBROT, University of Warsaw
POST-DIGITAL ELECTRONICS
F. R. PETTIT, Computing Teaching Centre, Oxford
OPTICAL AND OPTOELECTRONIC DEVICES AND SYSTEMS
DOUGLAS A. ROSS, University of Colorado at Denver
HANDBOOK OF RECTIFIER CIRCUITS
G. J. SCOLES, formerly English Electric Valve Company, Chelmsford, Essex
PRINCIPLES OF COMPUTER COMMUNICATION NETWORK DESIGN
J. SEIDLER, Institute of Fundamentals of Informatics, Polish Academy of Sciences

ELECTRONIC AND COMMUNICATION ENGINEERING

TELECOMMUNICATIONS TECHNOLOGY
R. L. BREWSTER, University of Aston in Birmingham
SATELLITE BROADCASTING SYSTEMS: Planning and Design
J. N. SLATER, Independent Broadcasting Authority, Winchester and L. A. TRINOGGA, Leeds Polytechnic
SIGNAL CODING AND PROCESSING: An Introduction Based on Video Systems
J. G. WADE, Plymouth Polytechnic

PARALLEL ARRAY PROCESSING

P. G. DUCKSBURY, B.Sc., Ph.D.
Senior Programmer
Systems Designers Scientific
Gloucester

ELLIS HORWOOD LIMITED
Publishers · Chichester

Halsted Press: a division of
JOHN WILEY & SONS
New York · Chichester · Brisbane · Toronto

First published in 1986 by
ELLIS HORWOOD LIMITED
Market Cross House, Cooper Street,
Chichester, West Sussex, PO19 1EB, England
The publisher's colophon is reproduced from James Gillison's drawing of the ancient Market Cross, Chichester.

Distributors:
Australia and New Zealand:
JACARANDA WILEY LIMITED
GPO Box 859, Brisbane, Queensland 4001, Australia
Canada:
JOHN WILEY & SONS CANADA LIMITED
22 Worcester Road, Rexdale, Ontario, Canada
Europe and Africa:
JOHN WILEY & SONS LIMITED
Baffins Lane, Chichester, West Sussex, England
North and South America and the rest of the world:
Halsted Press: a division of
JOHN WILEY & SONS
605 Third Avenue, New York, NY 10158, USA

British Library Cataloguing in Publication Data
Ducksbury, P.G.
Parallel array processing. —
(Ellis Horwood series in electrical and electronic engineering)
1. Parallel processing (Electronic computers)
I. Title
004'.35 QA76.6

Library of Congress Card No. 86–2908

ISBN 0–7458–00019–X (Ellis Horwood Limited)
ISBN 0–470–20330–7 (Halsted Press)

Printed in Great Britain by R. J. Acford, Chichester

Contents

Acknowledgements

This book is based on research undertaken at the Hatfield Polytechnic under the supervision of Dr L. C. W. Dixon, Dr K. D. Patel and Mr D. J. Hunt of ICL. I would like to thank them for their help and support and would also like to mention the help of my colleague Patrick Dolan.

I would also like to thank the Distribution Array Processor Support Unit at Queen Mary College, University of London, on whose machine the research was carried out.

Finally I would like to acknowledge the Science and Engineering Research Council for their financial support.

CHAPTER 1

Introduction

In recent years with technological change and innovation the cost of computated processing power has dropped dramatically. Every few years, new, faster and cheaper processors become available; the advent of these cheap processors has led to their combination into a variety of parallel processing systems. This has challenged software designers to redesign software so that it could take advantage of the new parallel systems.

It should be recognised that the results presented in the following chapters clearly demonstrate that there are advantages to be gained in using a parallel processor. Certainly with new applications such as robotics, speech recognition, artificial intelligence, image processing, etc., the need for faster processing devices becomes more important. Sequential architectures are approaching an impassible barrier since instructions are executed serially one at a time. The physics of electronic devices imposes an absolute limit on the speed at which instructions can be pushed through this barrier; hence the only solution is to employ the new parallel systems such as those mentioned in Chapter 2. This chapter is primarily intended for readers who are not familar with parallel systems; it corners the range of parallel architectures that were available in 1981. With this in mind, Appendix 1 is intended to act as an introduction to implementing a parallel algorithim, in this case a global optimisation alorithm on the distributed array processor (DAP) built by ICL. One of the these machines has been installed at Queen Mary College, University of London. It will be seen from reading this appendix that the behaviour of parallel implementations of sequential codes on parallel hardware depends critically on a careful match between the innate parallelism of the problems, the algorithm and the hardware. Little is likely to be gained by attempting to use parallel processing on a problem that is essentially sequential or by attempting to use on a particular parallel processing system an algorithm in which any parallelism is of a totally different nature.

From the experience with Price's algorithm, (Appendix 1) the description of parallelism in the ICL DAP and the experience of another colleague, Dr P. Singh, it was decided to investigate the difficulties of solving two-dimensional partial differential equations (p.d.e.s) by the finite element optimisation approach on the ICL

DAP. It is intended that the results presented later in this book will justify that decision. The description of the ICL DAP system in Chapter 2 is therefore given in more detail than descriptions of other systems. Naturally it is easier to solve linear p.d.e.s than non-linear p.d.e.s, and it is of course easier to solve steady state p.d.e.s than those that include time variations. The decision was taken to investigate methods that solve both linear and non-linear problems but not to extend the solution method to the time-varying case.

The approach to the solution is by means of converting the problem into an equivalent optimisation problem and then discretising by introducing finite elements. The solution of the set of equations that arise will then be obtained by using a suitable parallel form of the conjugate gradient algorithm.

The solution of p.d.e.s. can be converted into an optimisation problem in two very different ways. Some p.d.e.s arise naturally from the minimization of a functional and are simply the Euler–Lagrange equations for that functional; these p.d.e.s. are also termed self-adjoint. When such a natural functional exists, the natural optimisation problem to take is simply the minimisation of that functional. When no such functional exists, then it is possible to create a family of functions whose minimum will correspond to the solution of the p.d.e.s by taking weighted least-squares integrals of the solution. Different weighting matrices give rise to different optimisation problems and different approximations to the solutions. Many variants of this approach have been adopted in the past by advocates of the least-squares finite element method for solving non-self-adjoint p.d.e.s; that described in Chapter 5 is only one amongst many.

The initial work on the DAP involved both linear and non-linear p.d.e.s; the linear system was self-adjoint and the natural functionals were used. These natural functionals are quadratic in the unknowns and hence optimisation was equivalent to solving a set of linear equations. For this a parallel form of linear conjugate gradients was used. In contrast, the non-linear p.d.e.s were not self-adjoint and so the least-squares was adopted. Two solution methods were investigated, the first a parallel implementation of the non-linear conjugate gradient optimisation algorithm of Fletcher and Reeves [1] and the second a parallel implementation of the truncated Newton algorithm, in which the sets of linear equations were solved by the linear conjugate gradient code developed earlier.

Whilst considerable effort has been expended in investigating a whole variety of sequential approaches to the solution of p.d.e.s, there is really remarkably little agreement on the relative merits of successful methods. The question of the relative merits of finite difference and finite element methods is still hotly debated; the approach adopted in this thesis is the finite element approach. Amongst finite element practioners, it is widely accepted that for self-adjoint linear systems the use of Galerkin's method is most efficient. It is also well known that the equations that then arise are identical with those that arise when minimising the natural functional approximated by the same finite elements. The relative efficiency of the sequential finite element optimisation method on this special subclass is therefore identical with Galerkin's method. For non-self-adjoint or non-linear problems there is no agreed winning method; that investigated at least has the property of resting on a convergent theory, namely that of unconstrained optimisation. The method introduces an optimisation function which is reduced steadily at each iteration. The necessary safeguards that must be introduced to guarantee termination in a finite number of iterations are well known and have been implemented in the code.

One of the difficulties encountered was the choice of alternative solution methods for comparison purposes. In each case a sequential code for The Hatfield Polytechnic's DEC–1091 was written using the same principles as those used on the DAP system. This was a natural basis for comparison of the direct benefits of the parallel system.

Some of the main difficulties in the solution of p.d.e.s are firstly that a p.d.e. can have a large freedom of formulation as in the Navier–Stokes equations, secondly that certain p.d.e.s may require individual treatment and thirdly that there exist many numerical methods for dealing with small classes of problems but none of them is truly universal.

Most of the effort in the field of p.d.e. software has been in the field of 'special-purpose codes'. These meet particular requirements and solve specific problems without reference to the mathematical formulation; they can usually be used by specialists of a particular field but are rarely available for use by research students.

We intend to show that p.d.e.s can be efficiently solved on a parallel computer by finite elements and conjugate gradients.

In Chapter 2 the basic categories of parallel computers that are available today will be described and the detailed structure of the DAP will be given in more detail, together with an overview of the programming style that it requires. The experience obtained using the DAP on Price's algorithm is given in Appendix 1. In Chapter 3 the basis of the finite element optimisation approach are given. In Chapter 4 the solution of the self-adjoint two-dimensional heat conduction equation is considered, followed in Chapter 5 by a description of the solution of a non-linear p.d.e. by the non-linear conjugate gradient method (Section 5.1) and by the truncated Newton method (Section 5.2).

Chapter 6 will describe how the masking facilities of the DAP can be used to solve problems that do not appear to map naturally onto the machine, whilst Chapter 7 contains the solution of a Navier–Stokes problem.

There are several additional appendixes to this work: Appendix 2 lists the available built-in functions of the DAP language, Appendix 3 describes some of the codes written for the machine, whilst Appendix 4 gives some mathematical explanations required in Chapter 7.

CHAPTER 2

Parallel Computers and Programming

2.1 INTRODUCTION

Flynn [1] divided parallel computers that operate on multiple data streams into two categories. They are multiple-instruction multiple-data (MIMD) machines and single-instruction multiple-data (SIMD) machines.

Each of the two categories has its own particular characteristics which will now be described. The MIMD machines will typically have a relatively small number of reasonably powerful processors all interconnected and capable of working either in unison or independently of each other. Hence it is possible for independent program tasks to be coded and allocated to individual processors, but extreme care must be taken when information is shared between the processors and in their synchronisation; for example, one processor may require as input the output from another processor. Obviously it is possible to visualise that, even with a considerable amount of planning and synchronisation, some processors may be sitting idle waiting for other processors to complete their tasks. An example of this type of machine is the Loughborough Neptune computer which is based on four Texas Instruments 990/10 minicomputers, described by Barlow *et al*. [2].

Data-flow computers, although MIMD machines, really require a separate subcategory as their approach is so different. These machines are based on an entirely new concept. In a standard sequential computer a program is represented by a serial list of instructions. In a MIMD computer, several sections of code can be executed in parallel on different processors. However, further parallelism may exist in each of these sections which may be hidden from the programmer inside individual program instructions. The data-flow approach relies on a directed graph representation which will now be briefly illustrated. Consider the equation

$$y = 2x^3 + 3x^2 + 4x + 5$$

which can of course be expressed as a single high level program expression in the conventional sense. This can be represented, however, by the directed graph shown in Fig. 2.1 where each of the

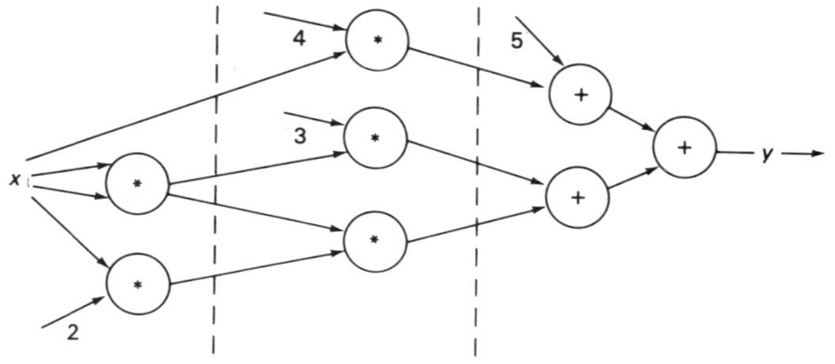

Fig. 2.1

nodes are basic operations. If these are linked by arrows representing the inputs–outputs, then the serial-parallel relationships become more apparent; a given node can perform its function only when all its inputs are available, and hence the control of operations is by *dataflow*. This approach to parallel exploitation does have the advantage of enabling the programmer to use a conventional language for implementation. Details of this type of approach have been given by Johnson *et al*. [3] and Sauber [4], both from Texas Instruments, and by da-Silva and Woods [5] using the Manchester machine.

In complete contrast the SIMD machines will usually have a large number (possibly thousands) of less powerful processors again interconnected (albeit more rigidly) but this time only capable of performing the same basic tasks.

Both vector pipeline and array processor machines are usually said to fall within this category. Typical examples are the CRAY-1 and ICL DAP respectively. The CRAY-1, however, does not possess a large number of processors but can be categorised as an SIMD machine since parallel operands are restricted to the same operation. To illustrate this pipelining effect, consider the floating point element by element multiplication of two vectors, x and y with the result being assigned to z (all vectors of length 64); to form each result in z we must carry out the following.

(1) Form the product of fractions.
(2) Add the exponents.
(3) Normalise and round the results.

In a simple sequential computer these three stages will be executed sequentially for each pair of operands. Note that, when performing the addition of the exponents at stage (2), then stage (1) is idle; similarly, when normalising results at stage (3), stages (1) and (2)

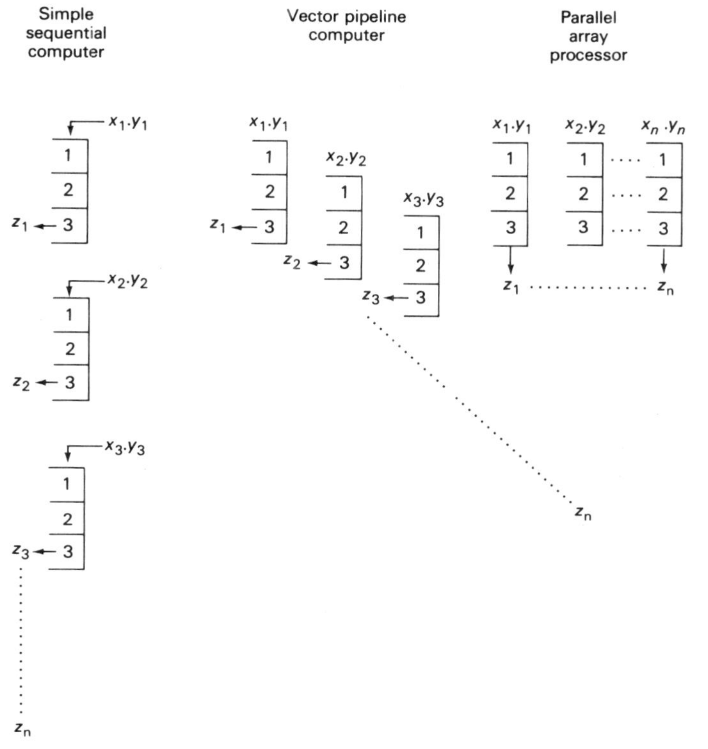

Fig. 2.2

are idle. In a vector pipeline machine such as the CRAY-1, there will be a number of segmented functional units that may proceed in parallel; for instance, when we have formed the product of fractions of x_1 and y_1, we commence adding the exponents of x_1 and y_1, but at the same time we start forming the product of fractions of x_2 and y_2, etc. (a medium or high speed sequential machine will also take advantage of this pipelining). This is illustrated in Fig. 2.2 ($n = 64$).

For the sequential case we require three clock pulses per result (giving a total of 192 pulses to form the complete vector z), and for the vector pipeline one clock pulse per result (after an initial two pulses, a total of 66 pulses; for comparison note that on an array processor we achieve all n results in just three clock pulses. Details of the CRAY-1 are available in [6] and [7].

It was considered that the MIMD computers available for use were inappropriate for the solution of p.d.e.s. or large dimensional optimisation problems that we wished to investigate; this left us with a choice of either array processors such as the ICL DAP or the vector pipeline processors such as the CRAY-1. Both of these machines have the ability to solve the problems of interest, but for the following reasons the ICL DAP was chosen as the machine to investigate. Firstly the DAP's grid of processors maps naturally onto the type of problems to be solved and secondly it implies a deeper study of the parallelism in the algorithm than the CRAY-1 which tends to conceal it from the user.

In section 2.2 we shall describe in further detail the structure of the DAP and the language DAP FORTRAN, and then in Chapter 3 we shall explain why we consider the DAP architecture suitable for the finite element optimisation solution of p.d.e.s.

2.2 THE DISTRIBUTED ARRAY PROCESSOR

The ICL DAP is an SIMD type of machine with its current version having a total of 4096 processors arranged in a 64×64 matrix structure. It does not form a stand-alone computer in its own right but acts as a store module which is linked to a conventional mainframe computer; a detailed description has been given by Reddaway [8].

The processors of an SIMD class of machine are usually very basic in their design when compared with those of an MIMD type of machine or of a mainframe computer. In the DAP the processors or rather the processing elements (PEs) are bit organised, which gives a great flexibility to the type of applications which are suited to it. These include image processing, data scanning and symbol processing in addition to basic arithmetic.

A basic sketch of the arrangement of the DAP is shown in Fig. 2.3. There we indicate that each PE is connected to its nearest four neighbours; there are also row and column data highways which connect all processors in a given row or column and allow for rapid broadcasting of information across the processing matrix. In addition to this facility we can connect the north–south–east–west boundaries to produce a cylinder or a torus depending upon the boundary connection chosen. In the machine at Queen Mary College, each processor has 16K bits of fast random access storage, giving a total store module of about 8M bytes; other installed machines have 4K bits per processor or 2M bytes in total.

Each PE is capable of independently holding its own data but they all receive the same common instructions which are broadcast from a master control unit (MCU), and hence the term SIMD.

Looking at the single PE in Fig. 2.4, we see that there are three registers, the activity A register which enables the processor to be

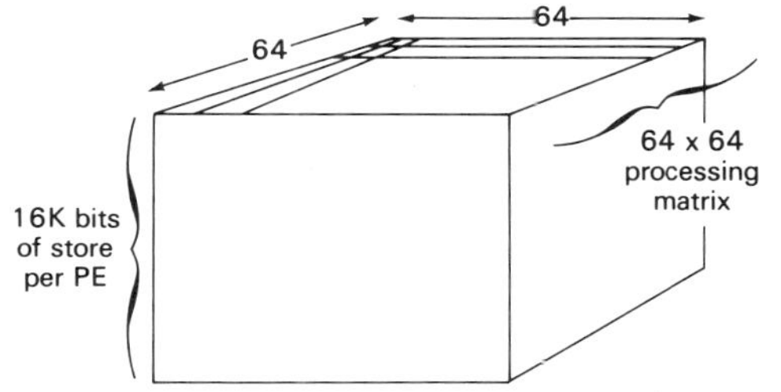

Fig. 2.3

deactivated if so required by the program, the Q register which is a 1-bit accumulator and the C register which acts as a carry store.

This ability to turn off a particular PE is of vital importance to the DAP; for instance, if we require to solve a problem with a grid size of less than 64×64, then the necessary PEs can quite simply be 'masked out' by means of a logical matrix, or we may wish to perform some mathematical operation on a matrix only where the individual matrix entries conform to certain requirements as will be illustrated later.

The programming of the DAP is by means of DAP FORTRAN which is an array processing extension of standard FORTRAN; details of the extension have been given by Flanders [9] and can be found in the official ICL manuals [10–12].

In standard FORTRAN the basic unit for computation is a scalar, but in DAP FORTRAN it can be a scalar, vector or matrix (where vectors and matrices have the dimensions N and $N \times N$ respectively,

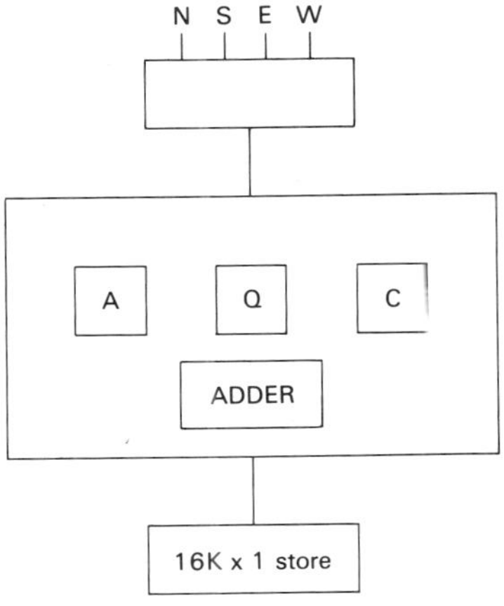

Fig. 2.4

N being the DAP size of 64). Hence the addition of two matrices in FORTRAN conventionally written as

```
      DO 10 I=1,N
      DO 10 J=1,N
        C(I,J)=A(I,J)+B(I,J)
10    CONTINUE
```

will in DAP FORTRAN be simply reduced to the single statement

```
C=A+B
```

The language DAP FORTRAN has a set of built-in functions for carrying out certain operations (details have been given in [11]; see also Appendix 2) such as the following.

SUM The scalar sum of an $N \times N$ matrix.
ABS The absolute value of every entry in an $N \times N$ matrix.
MAXV Finds the scalar maximum value in an $N \times N$ matrix.
MAXP Finds the position of the maximum value(s) in an $N \times N$ matrix, the position being indicated by a TRUE value in a logical matrix.
ALL This takes the logical AND of all values in an $N \times N$ logical matrix (or logical expression that delivers a logical matrix); this is extremely useful for a convergence test over a matrix, as will be illustrated later in this chapter.

The important facility of being able to switch off a particular processor by means of a logical matrix has previously been mentioned; a few examples of how this is used will now be given.

Assume that we have a matrix A which is 64×64 in size and contains positive and negative numbers, and the square root of all the positive entries only are required. This can be written in standard FORTRAN as

```
      DO 10 I=1,N
      DO 10 J=1,N
        IF(A(I,J) GT.O) A(I,J)=SQRT(A(I,J))
10    CONTINUE
```

which in DAP FORTRAN becomes

```
A(A.GT.O)=SQRT(A)
```

The expression A.GT.O. returns a logical matrix with TRUE values where A is greater than zero and FALSE values elsewhere. The result of the expression on the right-hand side is a matrix and the assignment is carried out only if the corresponding logical value on the left-hand side is TRUE; should this value be FALSE, then there will be no assignment at that position. To look at a more complicated example, let us take the solution of Laplace's equation, where we wish to replace each value in the matrix by the average of its four nearest neighbours. In standard FORTRAN we would write the code as

```
      DO 10 I=2,N−1
      DO 10 J=2,N−1
        Y(I,J)=(X(I+1,J)+X(I−1,J)+X(I,J+1)+X(I,J−1))/4
10    CONTINUE
```

and special code needs to be written to cope with the boundary of the matrix (that is avoiding a matrix subscript out of range error). The DAP FORTRAN can be expressed in the single statement

```
      X=(X(+,)+X(−,)+X(,+)+X(,−))/4
```

Here we make use of the shift indexing facilities of the DAP, where X(+,) will access the point on the neighbouring row of the PE matrix (corresponding to X(I+1,J) in the serial version), X(−,) will access the point on the preceding row etc. It is important to note that all points in the matrix are updated simultaneously (avoiding the need for an additional matrix for the result) and the boundaries of the matrix are handled automatically with zeros being shifted in; this depends of course on the geometry being used. With plane geometry, zeros are shifted in but, with cyclic geometry, we can link either the north–south or the east–west edges (to produce a cylinder) dependent on the implied direction of shift or we could link all four to produce a torus.

Suppose now that we wished to solve Laplace's problem over an irregularly shaped boundary (or a rectangular domain less than 64×64 in size); DAP FORTRAN permits us to create a logical matrix called DOMAIN, say, and then to assign TRUE values in the required part of the matrix to correspond to the domain of the problem and FALSE values elsewhere in the matrix. The code for the solution becomes

```
      DO 10 I=I,LIMIT
        OLDX=X
        X(DOMAIN)=(X(+,)+X(−,)+X(,+)+X(,−))/4
      IF(ALL(ABS(X−OLDX).LT.EPS)) GOTO 20
10    CONTINUE
      CONVERGED=.FALSE.
      RETURN
20    CONVERGED=.TRUE.
      RETURN
```

This chapter has described briefly the nature of the ICL DAP and the style of programming that it requires. In the following chapters we shall describe the solution of both linear and non-linear p.d.e.s on the DAP (and give further details of the DAP implementations in the appendix). In particular, in Chapter 3 we shall describe why we consider the DAP to be extremely suitable for solving p.d.e.s by the finite element conjugate gradient optimisation approach.

CHAPTER 3

Finite Element Optimisation

3.1 INTRODUCTION

In this chapter the reasons for choosing the finite element optimisation approach for solving these problems will be described.

As mentioned in Chapter 1, certain p.d.e.s arise naturally from the minimisation of a functional. Consider the optimisation problem

$$\min I = \int_V F[u(x)]\, \mathrm{d}V \tag{3.1}$$

subject to some appropriate boundary conditions; then the conditions for the minimum of (1.1) are Euler–Langrange equations which will be a set of partial differential equations. Now if the function F depends only on u and $\dot{u}$ where $\dot{u}$ is defined as

$$\dot{u} = \frac{\partial u}{\partial x} \tag{3.2}$$

then the equations become

$$\frac{\partial F}{\partial u} - \frac{\partial}{\partial x}\left(\frac{\partial F}{\partial \dot{u}}\right) = 0 \tag{3.3}$$

Hence, in order to solve the p.d.e. (3.3) subject to some boundary conditions, we may minimise (3.1) subject to those conditions. P.d.e.s that are associated with this class are termed self-adjoint.

For the non-self-adjoint problems, where a functional does not exist a function can be created whose minimum will correspond to the solution of the p.d.e. Suppose the non-self-adjoint set of p.d.e.s can be rearranged as a set of first-order p.d.e.s

$$e\left(\frac{\partial \mathbf{u}}{\partial x}, \mathbf{u}, \mathbf{x}\right) = 0 \tag{3.4}$$

then the solution of these equations subject to a set of boundary conditions occurs at the minimum of

$$I = \iint_V \mathbf{e}^{\mathrm{T}} \cdot w\, \mathbf{e}\, \mathrm{d}V \tag{3.5}$$

subject to the same conditions, where W is any positive definite symmetric operator.

3.2 INTRODUCING THE FINITE ELEMENTS

When using the finite element approach, the domain V is covered by a set of grid points x and then divided into a set of elements v_i having grid points at the intersections. For reasons of simplicity, rectangular elements were chosen; these map naturally onto the DAP's processor grid and therefore for each element v_i a set of four bi-linear shape functions $\phi(x)$ is introduced defined by

$$\phi_{ki}(x) = \frac{[1 - (x_{k,1} \pm x_1)/h][1 - (x_{k,2} \pm x_2)/h]}{4} \tag{3.6}$$

such that

$$\phi_{ki}(x) = 1 \text{ at } x_k \in V_i$$

$\phi_{ki}(x) = 0$ at x_j for $j \neq k, x_j \in v_i$ and at all points $x \in V_i$ and in each element V_i each unknown variable $u(x)$ is approximated by a linear combination

$$u(x) = \sum_k U_k \phi_{ki}(x) \tag{3.7}$$

where U_k is the value of $u(x)$ at the node x_k and the summation is formed over the four local nodes of the element.

By substituting the approximation (3.7) into equation (3.1) we obtain

$$\min I = \int F\left[\sum_k U_k \phi_{ki}(x)\right] \mathrm{d}V \tag{3.8}$$

The function I in equation (3.8) will now have a stationary point at the solution of the set of equations

$$g_k(U) = \frac{\partial I}{\partial U_k} = 0 \tag{3.9}$$

and will be a minimum if the Hessian matrix G is positive definite, where G is defined by

$$G_{ki}(U) = \frac{\partial^2 I}{\partial U_k \, \partial U_i} \tag{3.10}$$

For the non-self-adjoint problem the approximation (3.7) will be substituted into equation (3.5), once the expressions for the vector e have been derived. These expressions for e will of course be problem dependent as will be seen in Chapters 5 and 7.

3.3 MAPPING ONTO THE DAP

Let us consider the DAP's grid of processors, and allocate one element to each processor in the same manner in which the elements occur within the problem. Hence, because of the DAP's existing rectangular structure, the decision was taken to use rectangularly shaped elements. Triangular elements could also have been mapped onto the DAP quite effectively; however, this would have required some slightly more complicated code.

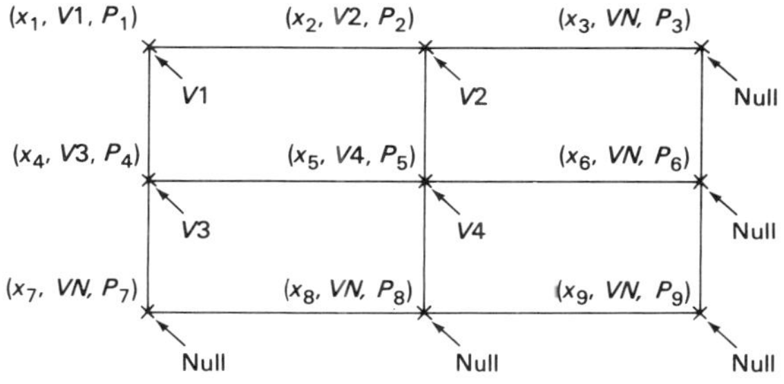

Fig. 3.1

Consider Figure 3.1, with a 3×3 grid and a 2×2 set of elements. The global mapping of grid points x_k and elements V_i onto the processor's P_k, is to be denoted in the form (x_k, V_i, P_k). All the element information is stored on the uppermost left processor which is associated with that element; consequently the last row and column of element storage is unused(denoted by V_N). Having obtained the element information and having stored it locally, we now perform the finite element calculations for each element V_i. All these calculations for element V_i will be performed in parallel with those of the remaining elements.

It is this fact that forms the DAP's most significant advantage over sequential computers, which typically will have to evaluate each element V_i sequentially.

3.4 ACCURACY OF THE SOLUTION

To derive a bound for the accuracy of this approach consider taking the following three functions.

(1) $u(x)$, the exact solution, the value of I being denoted by I^*, and the value of u by $u^*(x)$.
(2) The minimum of (3.8) denoted by I_m, and the minimum u by u_m.
(3) The linear interpolation denoted by I_1, with $U_1 = u^*(x)$.

The approximate minimum I_m must be worse than the exact minimum I^* and better than the interpolated solution; so

$$I^* \leqslant I_m \leqslant I_i$$

Let $u_i(x) = \Sigma\, U_I \phi_i(x)$ where $u = U_I$ at vertices; then let M be an upper bound on $\partial^2 u^* / \partial x_i\, \partial x_j$ and therefore

$$\| u^* - u_I \| \leqslant \tfrac{1}{2} M r_{el}^2$$

where r_{el} is the maximum element size. Thus if K is a suitable bound on the first derivative of

$$\frac{\partial F}{\partial u} (u^*)$$

then by the Taylor series we can derive the following relationship:

$$F(u_I) - F(u^*) < \tfrac{1}{2} K M r_{el}^2$$

Therefore

$$\int [F(u_I) - F(u^*)]\, dA < \tfrac{1}{2} K M r_{el}^2 \mathrm{A}$$

but there exists a k such that $r_{el} < kh$, for $k < 1$. We now have the relationship

$$I_I \leqslant I^* + \tfrac{1}{2} K M A k^2 h^2$$

and it also follows that

$$I_m \leqslant I^* + \tfrac{1}{2} K M A k^2 h^2$$

If F is quadratic in u, ∇u then $I(U)$ becomes the quadratic function

$$I(U) = \tfrac{1}{2} U^T A U + b^T U + c$$

and since $\partial I / \partial U = AU + b$ then, at the minimum, $AU = -b$. Therefore

$$I_I - I_m = \tfrac{1}{2}(U_I - U_m)^T A (U_I - U_m)$$

and

$$(U_I - U_m)^T A (U_I - U_m) \leqslant K M A k^2 h^2$$

Finally

$$\| U_I - U_m \|^2 \leqslant \frac{K M V A k^2 h^2}{mA}$$

where mA is the smallest eigenvalue of A.

In the next chapter a description of the solution method for the first class of p.d.e.s mentioned will be given, namely those which arise naturally from the minimisation of a functional. This will be followed in Chapter 5 by a description of the non-self-adjoint problem.

CHAPTER 4

The Linear Problem

4.1 INTRODUCTION

In this chapter the solution of the p.d.e.s that arise from the two-dimensional heat conduction equation will be described. These have been chosen as typical self-adjoint problems and were chosen because they have appeared so frequently in the literature.

The solution method follows the Galerkin finite element method. This would normally be solved on a sequential machine by first computing local stiffness matrices, then assembling them into a global stiffness matrix and finally solving the resulting sparse set of linear simultaneous equations.

In the implementation on the DAP the assembly of the global stiffness matrix is unnecessary and, as it was felt that this might be expensive in computer time when the method was extended to non-linear systems, it was therefore avoided. The set of unassembled linear equations was solved by the conjugate gradient algorithm. Again, as a preliminary to examining the non-linear systems where the equivalent optimisation problem is non-quadratic and its gradient non-linear, the rather different conjugate gradient code usually used to minimise non-quadratic functions was coded and tested on these problems.

4.2 THE PROBLEM

The two-dimensional heat conduction equation is given by

$$\frac{\partial}{\partial x}\left(K_x \frac{\partial T}{\partial x}\right) + \frac{\partial}{\partial y}\left(K_y \frac{\partial T}{\partial y}\right) = -Q \tag{4.1}$$

where K_x and K_y are thermal conductivities in the x and y directions, Q is the local heat source or sink, T is the unknown temperature, and x and y are the distance coordinates. It is well known that the solution to equation (4.1) will occur at the minimum of

$$I = \iint \left[K_x \left(\frac{\partial T}{\partial x}\right)^2 + K_y \left(\frac{\partial T}{\partial y}\right)^2 - 2QT\right] \mathrm{d}V \tag{4.2}$$

as was described in Chapter 3. For such problems the objective becomes one of solving

$$\min I = \int F[T(x)]\, \mathrm{d}V \tag{4.3}$$

subject to the appropriate boundary conditions.

By introducing finite elements the domain V is covered by a set of grid points x_k and then divided into a set of elements V_i with grid points at intersections; for each element there are shape functions ϕ_{ki} such that

$$\phi_{ki}(x) = 1 \text{ at } x_k$$

$$\phi_{ki}(x) = 0 \text{ at } x_j \text{ for } j \neq k \text{ and at all points } x \in V_i$$

It is now possible to approximate *T(x)* by a linear combination of the shape functions:

$$\sum_k T_k \phi_{ki}(x) \tag{4.4}$$

so that equation (4.3) becomes approximately

$$\min I = \int F\left[\sum_k T_k \phi_{ki}(x)\right] \mathrm{d}V \tag{4.5}$$

On substituting (4.4) into equation (4.2), we get

$$F(T) = \iint \left[K_x \left(\sum_i \frac{\partial \phi_i}{\partial x} T_i \right)^2 + K_y \left(\sum_i \frac{\partial \phi_i}{\partial y} T_i \right)^2 - 2Q \sum_i \phi_i T_i \right] \mathrm{d}V \tag{4.6}$$

and, on differentiating this with respect to T_i, we obtain g_i:

$$\begin{aligned} g_i &= \nabla F_i(T) \\ &= \iint \left[2K_x \frac{\partial \phi_i}{\partial x} \left(\sum_j \frac{\partial \phi_j}{\partial x} T_j \right) + 2K_y \frac{\partial \phi_i}{\partial y} \left(\sum_j \frac{\partial \phi_j}{\partial y} T_j \right) - 2Q \sum_i \phi_i \right] \mathrm{d}V = 0 \end{aligned} \tag{4.7}$$

Differentiating once more gives $\nabla^2 F_{ij}$:

$$\nabla^2 F_{ij}(T) = \iint \left(2K_x \frac{\partial \phi_i}{\partial x} \frac{\partial \phi_j}{\partial x} + 2K_y \frac{\partial \phi_i}{\partial y} \frac{\partial \phi_j}{\partial y} \right) \mathrm{d}V \tag{4.8}$$

When the Q_i values represent point sources at the nodes, then they can be moved outside the integration; thus equation (4.6) becomes

$$F(T) = \sum_{\text{el}} \iint_{\text{el}} \left[K_x \left(\sum_i \frac{\partial \phi_i}{\partial x} T_i \right)^2 + K_y \left(\sum_i \frac{\partial \phi_i}{\partial y} T_i \right) \right] \mathrm{d}V - 2Q_i T_i \tag{4.9}$$

equation (4.7) becomes

$$g_{i\,\text{el}} = \nabla F_i(T)_{\text{el}} = \iint_{\text{el}} \left[2K_x \frac{\partial \phi_i}{\partial x} \left(\sum \frac{\partial \phi_j}{\partial x} T_j \right) + 2K_y \frac{\partial \phi_i}{\partial y} \left(\sum \frac{\partial \phi_j}{\partial y} T_j \right) \right] \mathrm{d}V - 2Q_i = 0 \tag{4.10}$$

and equation (4.8) becomes

$$\nabla^2 F_{ij}(T) = \iint_{\text{el}} \left[2K_x \frac{\partial \phi_i}{\partial x} \frac{\partial \phi_j}{\partial x} + 2K_y \frac{\partial \phi_i}{\partial y} \frac{\partial \phi_j}{\partial y} \right] \mathrm{d}V \tag{4.11}$$

The solution of problem (4.5) now becomes equivalent to the solution of equations (4.7). In section 4.3 we shall describe an approach which allows us to solve the system of equations $A\mathbf{u} = \mathbf{f}$ without having to form the global matrix A.

4.3 SOLUTION OF THE EQUATIONS

Once having derived the system of equations, it is necessary to solve them with a minimum amount of overhead.

Consider the system

$$A\mathbf{t} = \mathbf{f} \tag{4.12}$$

where A is an $N \times N$ real matrix, $\mathbf{t}$ an N unknown vector and $\mathbf{f}$ an N known vector. If N is large, a problem exists with computer storage. In the finite element approach the matrix A will be held as

$$\sum_{e=1}^{E} A^e$$

namely the sum of all the elements matrices.

All the values in a given A^e will be zero except for those occurring in rows on columns corresponding to variables in the element e.

It is therefore possible to solve the above system of equations (4.12) without having to assemble the original matrix A.

Consider the product

$$\mathbf{y} = A\mathbf{x} \tag{4.13}$$

This would in fact be calculated on an element-by-element basis, as

$$\mathbf{y}^e = A^e\mathbf{x}^e \tag{4.14}$$

where A^e is the element matrix for element V_i, $\mathbf{x}^e$ is a subset of $\mathbf{x}$ containing the four nodal values which are local to element V_i and $\mathbf{y}^e$ is a subset of $\mathbf{y}$ containing the four resultant values which are also local to element V_i these four values must be used to form the correct contributions to the global vector $\mathbf{y}$, (which is itself a comparatively simple operation on the DAP).

The solution of the system of equations was undertaken by adapting the conjugate gradient method. The conjugate gradient method is an iterative method which converges to the correct solution of a set of linear equations in a finite number of iterations, assuming no rounding errors. The method was originally put forward by Hestenes and Stiefel in 1952 [1] and subsequently modified for non-linear optimisation by Fletcher and Reeves in 1964 [2]. In section 4.4 we shall describe an implementation of a linear conjugate gradient algorithm and show that DAP is an efficient machine for dealing with these types of problems, in Section 4.5 we shall describe a non-linear approach to the solution.

4.4 LINEAR CONJUGATE GRADIENT ALGORITHM

The basic linear conjugate gradient algorithm used is described below; note that we are solving the set of equations $A\mathbf{t} = \mathbf{f}$, using the following steps.

(1) Evaluate the equations A.
(2) Choose a suitable initial vector $\mathbf{t}^{(0)}$.
(3) Set $\mathbf{p}^{(0)} = \mathbf{t}^{(0)}$.
(4) Evaluate $\mathbf{w}^{(0)} = A\mathbf{p}^{(0)}$.
(5) Evaluate $\mathbf{f}^{(1)} = \mathbf{t}^{(0)} - \mathbf{w}^{(0)}$.
(6) If $\mathbf{f}^{(1)\mathrm{T}} \cdot \mathbf{f}^{(1)}$ is less than the tolerance, then *stop*.
(7) Set $\mathbf{p}^{(1)} = \mathbf{f}^{(1)}$ and $k = 1$.
(8) Evaluate $\mathbf{w}^{(k)} = A\mathbf{p}^{(k)}$.
(9) If $\mathbf{p}^{(k)\mathrm{T}} \cdot \mathbf{w}^{(k)}$ is less than the tolerance, then *stop*.
(10) Set the step length

$$\alpha^{(k)} = \frac{\mathbf{f}^{(k)\mathrm{T}} \cdot \mathbf{f}^{(k)}}{\mathbf{p}^{(k)\mathrm{T}} \cdot \mathbf{w}^{(k)}}$$

(11) Update the unknown

$$\mathbf{t}^{(k+1)} = \mathbf{t}^{(k)} + \alpha^{(k)}\mathbf{p}^{(k)}$$

and

$$\mathbf{f}^{(k+1)} = \mathbf{f}^{(k)} - \alpha^{(k)}\mathbf{w}^{(k)}$$

(12) If $\mathbf{f}^{(k+1)\mathrm{T}} \cdot \mathbf{f}^{(k+1)}$ is less than the tolerance, then *stop*.
(13) Set

$$\beta^{(k)} = \frac{\mathbf{f}^{(k+1)\mathrm{T}} \cdot \mathbf{f}^{(k+1)}}{\mathbf{f}^{(k)\mathrm{T}} \cdot \mathbf{f}^{(k)}}$$

(14) Update the search direction $\mathbf{p}$:

$$\mathbf{p}^{(k+1)} = \mathbf{f}^{(k+1)} + \beta^{(k)}\mathbf{p}^{(k)}$$

(15) Set $k = k + 1$; go to step (8).

As it was intended later to solve non-linear p.d.e.s which lead to a more non-linear function I, a non-linear conjugate gradient algorithm was also written and tested at this stage.

4.5 THE NON-LINEAR CONJUGATE GRADIENT ALGORITHM

This non-linear alogirthm is due to Fletcher and Reeves [2]; it can be summarised in the following steps.

(1) Initially guess vector $\mathbf{t}^{(1)}$; set $k = 1$.
(2) Evaluate stiffness matrices $\nabla^2 F$ $(=A)$ (this is not usually required but was included initially to test the remainder of the algorithm).
(3) Evaluate $\nabla F^{(k)}$ $(= g^{(k)})$.
(4) If $\mathbf{g}^{(k)\mathrm{T}} \cdot \mathbf{g}^{(k)}$ is less than the tolerance, then stop.
(5) If $k = 1$, then set
$\mathbf{p}^{(k)} = -\mathbf{g}^{(k)}$
or else set

$$\beta^{(k)} = \frac{\mathbf{g}^{(k)\mathrm{T}} \cdot \mathbf{g}^{(k)}}{\mathbf{g}^{(k-1)T} \cdot \mathbf{g}^{(k-1)}}$$

and

$$\mathbf{p}^{(k)} = -\mathbf{g}^{(k)} + \beta^{(k)}\mathbf{p}^{(k-1)}$$

(6) Evaluate $\alpha^{(k)}$ as $\alpha^{(k)} = \arg\min(F + \alpha\mathbf{p})$.
(7) Update the unknown $\mathbf{t}$ as $\mathbf{t}^{(k+1)} = \mathbf{t}^{(k)} + \alpha^{(k)}\mathbf{p}^{(k)}$.
(8) Set $k = k + 1$.
(9) If $k \leqslant k_{\max}$, then go to step (3) of else stop.

Additional costs can be expected at step (3) when the gradient vector is recalculated at each iteration by entering the finite element procedure rather than updated as in the linear algorithm. It should also be noted that at step (6) the Fletcher–Reeves algorithm would normally contain a line search for finding the step length α but, when doing comparison runs on quadratic functions, α is known analytically.

The expression for α comes from the following Taylor expansion:

$$F(T + \alpha\mathbf{p}) = F(T) + \alpha(\mathbf{g}^{\mathrm{T}} \cdot \mathbf{p}) + \frac{\alpha^2\mathbf{p}^{\mathrm{T}} \cdot A\mathbf{p}}{2}$$

And there will be a minimum of F when $\partial F/\partial\alpha = 0$. Hence

$$\frac{\partial F}{\partial \alpha} = \mathbf{g}^{\mathrm{T}} \cdot \mathbf{p} + \alpha\mathbf{p}^{\mathrm{T}} \cdot A\mathbf{p}$$

and therefore

$$\alpha = \frac{-\mathbf{g}^{\mathrm{T}} \cdot \mathbf{p}}{\mathbf{p}^{\mathrm{T}} \cdot A\mathbf{p}}$$

In later tests on non–linear functions, step(2) was omitted and step (6) was replaced by an iterative line search.

4.6 FORM OF THE CALCULATIONS

The products that need to be evaluated in the linear algorithm are as follows.

(1) $\mathbf{f}$, $\mathbf{t}$, $\mathbf{R}$.
(2) $\mathbf{f}^{\mathrm{T}} \cdot \mathbf{f}$, $\mathbf{p}^{\mathrm{T}} \cdot A\mathbf{p}$, evaluated as $\mathbf{p}^{\mathrm{T}} \cdot \mathbf{w}$.
(3) $\mathbf{w} = A\mathbf{p}$.

The products for the non-linear algorithm are as follows.

(1) $\mathbf{t}$, $\mathbf{R}$, $\mathbf{g}$.
(2) $\mathbf{g}^{\mathrm{T}} \cdot \mathbf{g}$, $\mathbf{g}^{\mathrm{T}} \cdot \mathbf{p}$.
(3) $\mathbf{p}^{\mathrm{T}} \cdot A\mathbf{p}$.

The calculations involved in the algorithms are based on information which is associated with each of the *elements*. For each element there is a 4×1 vector of values $\mathbf{g}^e$ used to form $\mathbf{g}$, a 4×1 vector of values $\mathbf{p}^e$ used to form $\mathbf{p}$ and a 4×4 matrix of values A^e, its local stiffness matrix. The values of $\mathbf{p}$, $\mathbf{g}$ and $\mathbf{f}$ at each grid point need to be calculated. The way in which this is achieved is to add contributions of the elements that are associated with a particular node, normally four elements for each node (but for a boundary node just two, or one for a corner node). The local node and element numbering is as described in Figs 4.1 and 4.2.

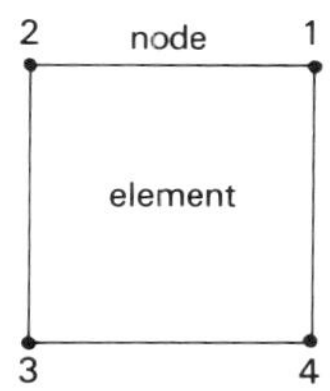

Fig. 4.1

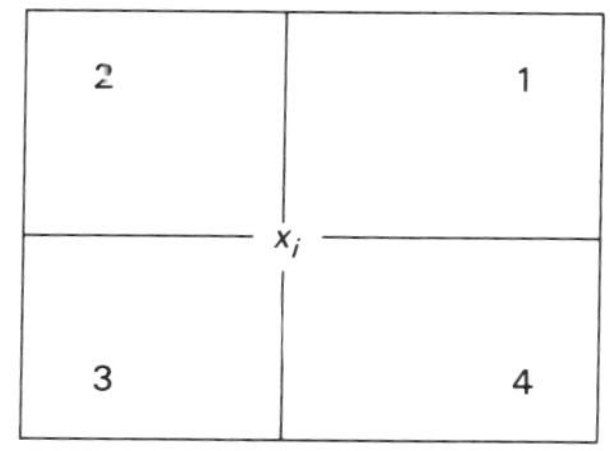

Fig. 4.2

To form p_i at node x_i,

$$p_i = \sum_{\text{el}=1}^{4} p_j^{\text{el}}$$

where j is the local node in element el which corresponds to the global node i, that is take the third value of p from element 1 plus the fourth value of p from element 2 plus the first value of p from element 3 plus the second value of p from element 4. The calculations are as follows.

(1) First we obtain

$$p_i = \sum_{\text{el}=1}^{4} p_j^{\text{el}}, \qquad g_i = \sum_{\text{el}=1}^{4} g_j^{\text{el}}, \qquad f_i = \sum_{\text{el}=1}^{4} f_j^{\text{el}},$$

and then

$$\mathbf{f}^{\mathrm{T}} \cdot \mathbf{f} = \sum_{i=1}^{N} f_i^2$$

A similar argument applies for $\mathbf{p}^{\mathrm{T}} \cdot \mathbf{p}$, $\mathbf{g}^{\mathrm{T}} \cdot \mathbf{g}$ and $\mathbf{g}^{\mathrm{T}} \cdot \mathbf{p}$.

(2) The product $A\mathbf{p}$ can be evaluated as

$$A\mathbf{p} = \sum_{j=1}^{4} \sum_{k=1}^{4} A_{jk}^{\text{el}} p_k$$

for el $= 1, \ldots, E$. In each element the four values of the resulting vector are placed back at the correct local nodes.

(3) The product $\mathbf{p}^{\mathrm{T}} \cdot A\mathbf{p}$ can be elevated as

$$\mathbf{p}^{\mathrm{T}} \cdot A\mathbf{p} = \sum_{\text{el}=1}^{E} \left(\sum_{j=1}^{4} \sum_{k=1}^{4} p_j A_{jk}^{\text{el}} p_k \right)$$

Full details of how the algorithms are mapped onto the DAP are given in Appendix 3; in section 4.7 we shall describe the conditions under which the algorithms were tested.

4.7 RESULTS

4.7.1 Introduction

The equation was solved for meshes of various sizes with appropriate point sources and point sinks; Table 4.1 at the illustrates the relative locations and strengths of these points. We shall now describe the boundary conditions used and the thermal conductivities.

Table 4.1 Locations and strengths of the source or sink points.

Grid size	Location				
11 × 11	(2, 2)	(2, 10)	(8, 2)	(6, 6)	(10, 10)
21 × 21	(2, 2)	(2, 20)	(14, 3)	(10, 11)	(20, 20)
31 × 31	(3, 3)	(3, 27)	(23, 4)	(14, 15)	(27, 27)
41 × 41	(6, 6)	(6, 36)	(28, 6)	(20, 20)	(36, 36)
64 × 64	(9, 9)	(9, 60)	(54, 9)	(34, 34)	(60, 60)
Q	1.0	0.5	0.6	−1.83	−0.27

In this and the following tables, all the sequential runs were performed on a DEC 1091 mainframe at Hatfield Polytechnic (this machine being approximatly 2.8 times slower than the ICL 2980 mainframe installed at Queen Mary College).

4.7.2 Boundaries

In Chapter 3 we mentioned that one condition for the minimum of

$$I = \int F(\dot{u}, u, x)\, \mathrm{d}V$$

was given by the Euler–Lagrange equations

$$\frac{\partial F}{\partial u} - \frac{\partial}{\partial x}\left(\frac{\partial F}{\partial \dot{u}}\right) = 0$$

The full analysis by the calculus of variations implies certain boundary conditions, namely that, if u is specified at the boundary, then these constraints must be imposed on both the minimum and the Euler–Lagrange equations. If these constraints are not imposed, then the minimum of I will correspond to natural boundary conditions of the form

$$\frac{\partial F}{\partial \dot{u}} = 0$$

For the function (4.2) this implies that, on the boundaries limiting x, $\partial \mathrm{T}/\partial \mathrm{x} = 0$ and, on those limiting y, $\partial \mathrm{T}/\partial y = 0$ unless T was specified.

In the results presented, the temperature T was only prescribed at one point on the boundary and therefore by implication the other boundary values imposed were $\partial T/\partial n = 0$. The fixed temperature was given the value of 1 and the matrix A was modified such that had it been assembled the corresponding row would have been equal to the identity, thus elminating one of the unknown equations from our system.

4.7.3 Conductivities

Four different conductivity distributions were used in the tests. They were specified independently in the x and y directions and located at the centre of an element.

PROBLEM 1

This is the *model problem* with K_x and K_y equal to unity over the entire region.

PROBLEM 2

This is the *generalized model problem* with K_x and K_y both constant, but with K_x 100 times greater in magnitude than K_y.

PROBLEM 3

This is the *heterogenous test problem*. Here the region was subdivided into a number of smaller regions; refer to Fig. 4.3 for the exact details of the subregions.

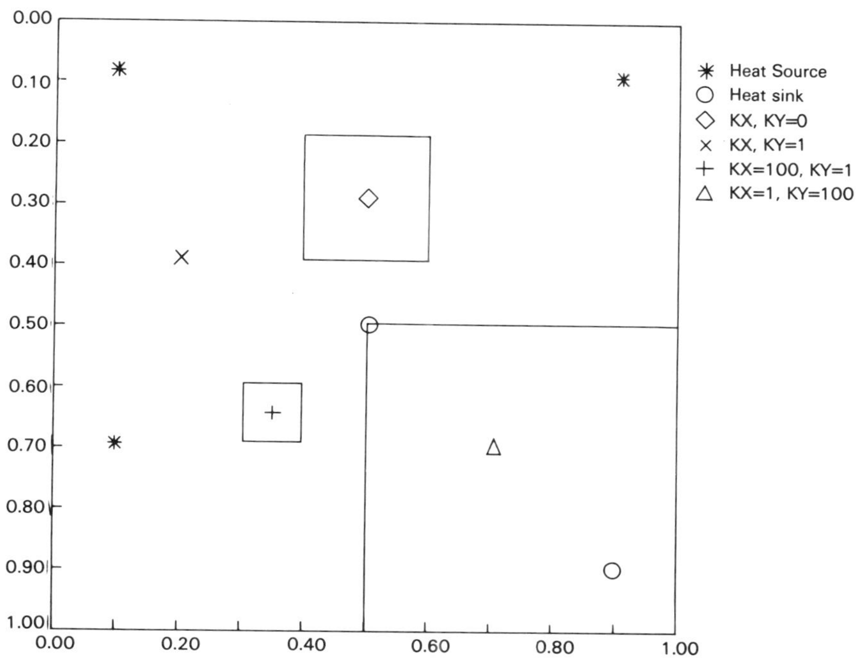

Fig. 4.3

PROBLEM 4

This was the same as for problem 3 except that, in one of the regions where K_x and K_y had been set to 1.0, the conductivities came via random numbers. The numbers were generated in the range (0, 1) and, if they were less than 0.1, then the conductivity in the x and y directions was set to zero, and otherwise to 1.0. This generates a large number of obstructions to heat flow.

This set of test functions is recognised as a standard test set and was used by Stone [4].

In section 4.7.4 we shall describe the numerical results that were obtained.

4.7.4 Numerical results

The numerical results obtained are divided into two sets depending on the algorithm used, that is the linear or non-linear version of the conjugate gradient algorithm. Those for the linear algorithm are given in Tables 4.2–4.5, and for the non-linear algorithm in Tables 4.6–4.9. The timings and the runs include the mesh generation as well as the solution by conjugate gradients. The results are more

Table 4.2 Problem 1 (linear), with K_x and K_y both equal to 1.0. Normal termination on $\sqrt{(\mathbf{f}^T \cdot \mathbf{f})} < 1e{-}6$.

N	Iterations		Time (s)	
	DEC	DAP	DEC	DAP
11	46	46	11.7	1.06
21	85	85	18.8	1.61
31	125	125	58.1	2.18
41	167	205	137.1	3.32
64	—	339	—	5.17

Table 4.3 Problem 2 (linear), with $K_x = 100$ and $K_y = 1$. Normal termination on $\sqrt{(\mathbf{f}^T \cdot \mathbf{f})} < 1e{-}6$.

N	Iterations		Time (s)	
	DEC	DAP	DEC	DAP
11	240	265	14.7	4.1
21	480	555	83.3	8.17
31	760	819	312.2	11.9
41	1060	1397	826.6	20.1
64	—	1768	—	24.09

Table 4.4 Problem 3 (linear), with K_x and K_y subdivided. Normal termination on $\sqrt{(\mathbf{f}^T \cdot \mathbf{f})} < 1e{-}6$.

N	Iterations		Time (s)	
	DEC	DAP	DEC	DAP
11	246	391	11.05	5.9
21	650	800	110.4	11.69
31	950	1481	354.0	21.34

Table 4.5 Problem 4 (linear), subdivided, with one random region. Normal termination on $\sqrt{(\mathbf{f})^T \cdot \mathbf{f})} < 1e{-}6$.

N	Iterations		Time (s)	
	DEC	DAP	DEC	DAP
11	260	403	12.03	6.1
21	875	880	153.5	12.79
31	1000	1400	359.8	20.15

Table 4.6 Problem 1 (non-linear), Normal termination on $\mathbf{g}^T \cdot \mathbf{g} < 1e{-}6$.

N	Iterations		Time (s)	
	DEC	DAP	DEC	DAP
11	38	37	33.0	6.9
21	70	70	255.9	12.5
31	100	101	758.4	18.2

Table 4.7 Problem 2 (non-linear), Normal termination on $\mathbf{g}^T \cdot \mathbf{g} < 1e{-}6$.

N	Iterations		Time (s)	
	DEC	DAP	DEC	DAP
11	156	147	75.7	26.6
21	298	288	1031.1	51.9
31	439	436	3277.2	78.5

Table 4.8 Problem 3 (non-linear). Normal termination on $\mathbf{g}^T \cdot \mathbf{g} < 1e{-}6$.

N	Iterations		Time (s)	
	DEC	DAP	DEC	DAP
11	242[a]	241	212.1	43.1
21	882[a]	609	3076.0	109.2
31	—	863	—	154.5

[a]The sequential algorithm failed to converge after $2N$ iterations, leaving a maximum gradient of 0.12 when the number of iterations was 242 and a maximum gradient of 0.18 when the number of iterations was 882 (N being the number of unknowns).

Table 4.9 Problem 4 (non-linear). Normal termination on $\mathbf{g}^T \cdot \mathbf{g} < 1e{-}6$.

N	Iterations		Time (s)	
	DEC	DAP	DEC	DAP
11	242[a]	257	217.0	45.8
21	—	664	—	118.2
31	—	904	—	161.0

[a]The sequential algorithm failed to converge after $2N$ iterations, leaving a maximum gradient of 0.012 (N being the number of unknowns).

easily represented in Graphs 4.1–4.7, where the logarithm of time has been plotted against grid size.

It is apparent from the graphs that the parallel implementations are considerably faster than the sequential ones; Graph 4.1 illustrates the solution process up to the full size of the DAP which was not possible on our sequential computer without resorting to backing store. The curves for the parallel case increase only slightly in comparison with those of the sequential case whose times soon become excessively large as the number of grid points increases or the ill conditioning gets worse. As we would expect, the times per iteration using the linear code are much lower than those obtained using the non-linear algorithm. We should also note that the non-linear tests were terminated earlier than the linear tests, that is on $\mathbf{g}^T \cdot \mathbf{g} < 1e - 6$ compared with $(\mathbf{f}^T \cdot \mathbf{f}) < 1e - 6$, as we only required an indication of the overhead involved in performing the global

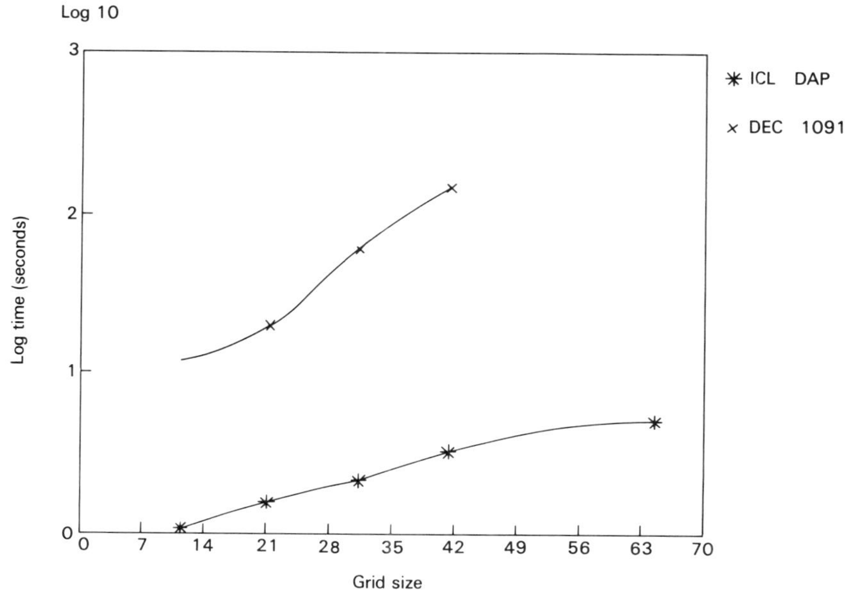

Graph 4.1 Problem 1 (linear).

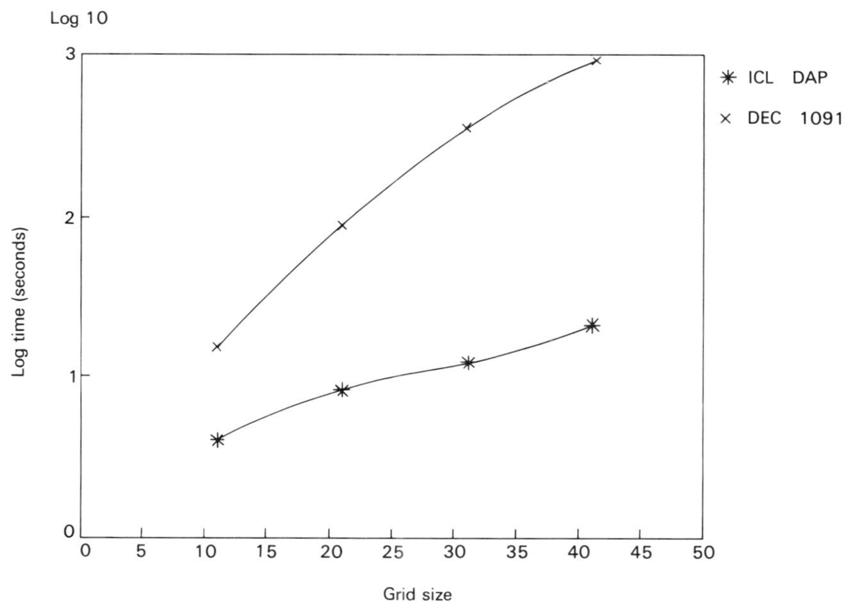

Graph 4.2 Problem 2 (linear).

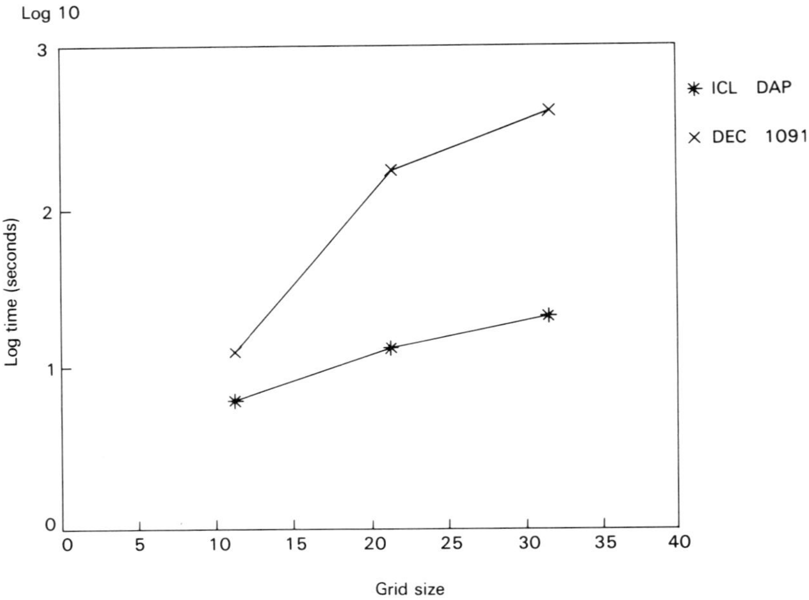

Graph 4.3 Problem 3 (linear).

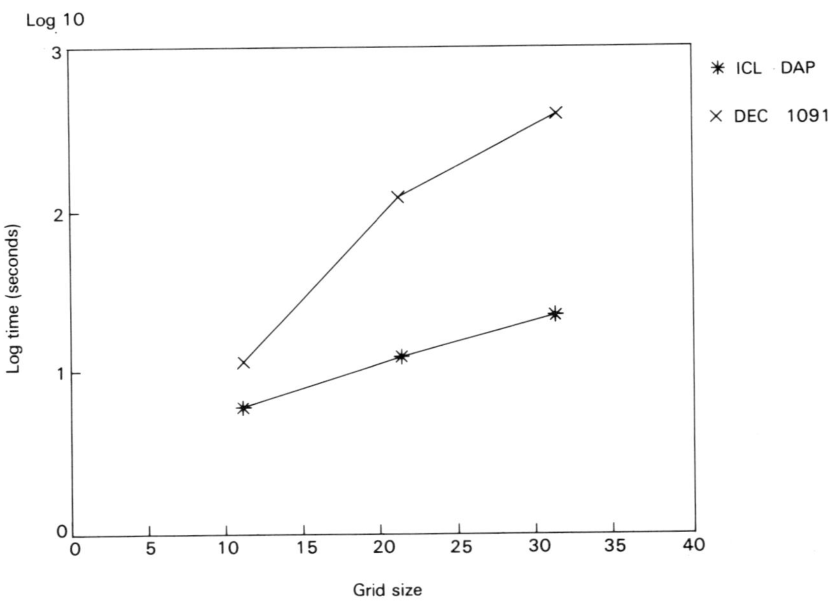

Graph 4.4 Problem 4 (linear).

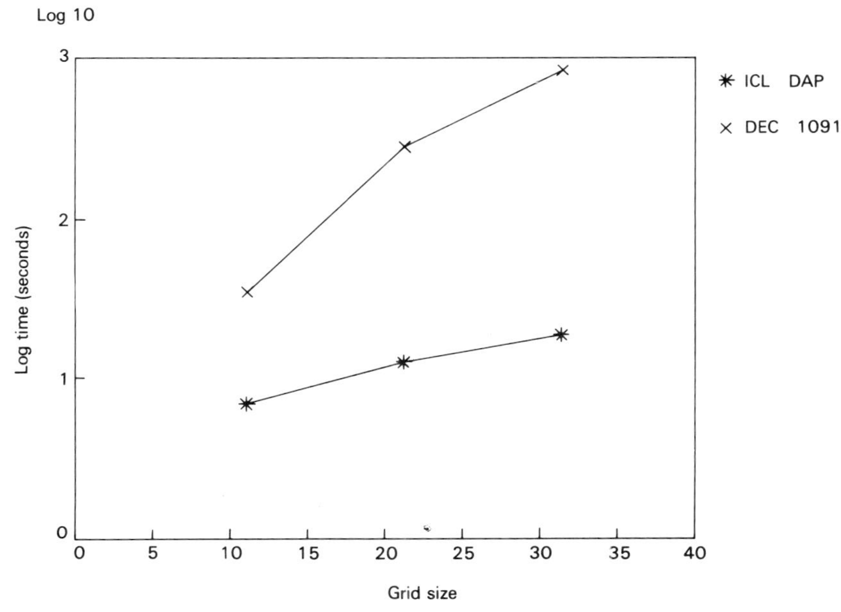

Graph 4.5 Problem 1 (non-linear).

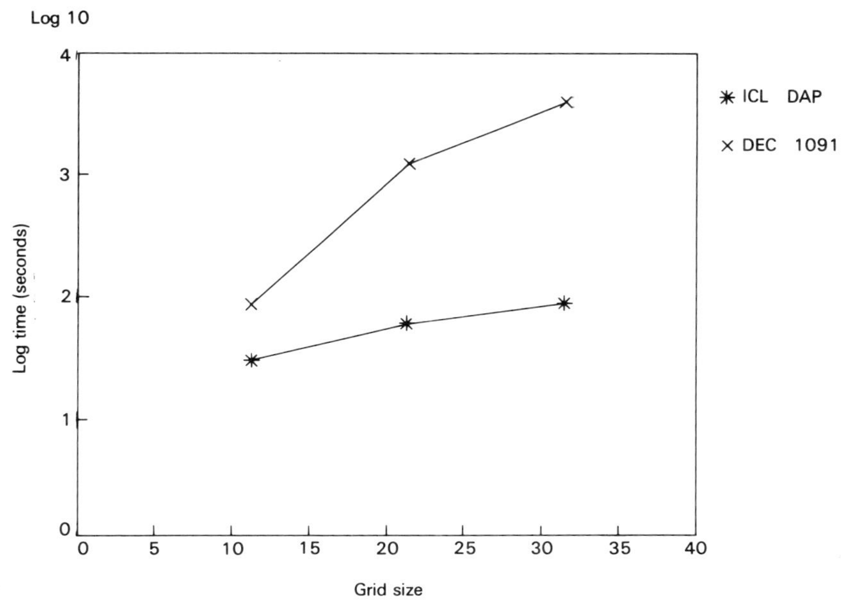

Graph 4.6 Problem 2 (non-linear).

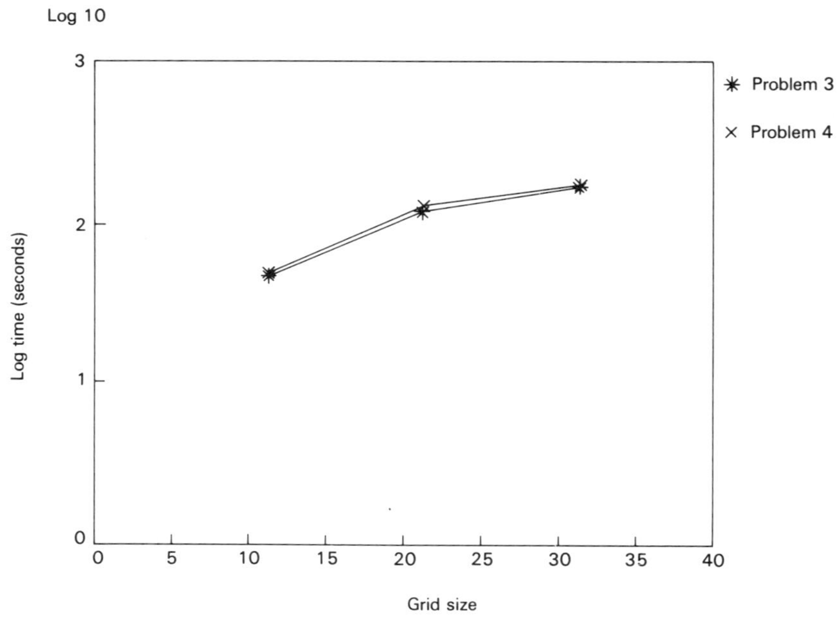

Graph 4.7 Problems 3 and 4 (non-linear).

calculations at every iteration. Comparing the iterations and time in Tables 4.2 and 4.6, this expense can clearly be seen.

The only unexpected results came from the non-linear sequential comparisons for problems 3 and 4. The resulting gradient failed to be significantly reduced and the iteration was stopped after $2N$ iterations (where N is the number of unknowns). The parallel algorithm terminated successfully, and this seems to imply that this implementation is much less affected by rounding error.

In section 4.7.5 shall briefly drawn together some conclusions about this work and this will be further expanded in the final discussion in Chapter 8.

4.7.5 Conclusions

The two parallel implementations have demonstrated the fact that the solution of p.d.e.s using this method of approach is very suitable for the DAP.

Almost certainly one of the main advantages of the DAP in this case was the fact that the processors are connected to their nearest four neighbours together with the powerful shift indexing facilities. We therefore have a very effective means for communicating with neighbouring elements and nodes. This facility can be compared with the complications necessary in the sequential programs which must keep, for each element, a separate record of the four neighbouring (local) nodes, which has to be set up and then repeatedly indexed for information.

If we examine Tables 4.2 and 4.3 in particular, it is noticeable that the implementation on the DAP achieves a maximum speed of up to 41 times that of the sequential version; this factor occurs at a grid size of 41×41 and we could naturally expect a larger factor had we been able to continue the sequential tests to the full DAP size.

This chapter has described the solution of a linear p.d.e. on the DAP. The natural extension of this work is the look at the solution of non-linear p.d.e.s; these will be described in Chapter 5.

CHAPTER 5

The Non-linear Problem

5.1 INTRODUCTION

In this chapter the implementation of the least-squares finite element method as used as part of the solution process for the non-linear Morgan problem will be described.

In the least-squares approach, two different mathematical formulations will be described in detail, followed by a description of the two different approaches to completing the solution, these being the non-linear conjugate gradient algorithm and the truncated Newton method.

5.2 THE PROBLEM

The sample problem chosen was the non-linear Morgan equation

$$\frac{\partial^2 u}{\partial x_1^2} + \frac{\partial^2 u}{\partial x_2^2} - Ru\frac{\partial u}{\partial x_1} = 0 \tag{5.1}$$

A solution to the equation is known, namely

$$u = \frac{6x_1}{Rx_2^2}$$

5.2.1 Solution by Least Squares: Formulation I

Using the least-squares finite element method the solution of the problem can be written as

$$\min I = \iint_V \mathbf{e}^{\mathrm{T}} \cdot W\mathbf{e}\ \mathrm{d}V \tag{5.2}$$

where $\mathbf{e} = e_1, e_2, \ldots, e_n)$ $(n = 3)$ and W is a diagonal weighting matrix $W_{ii} = \frac{1}{3}$ for $i = 1, \ldots, 3$. The minimisation is subject to some suitable boundary conditions.

By introducing

$$A = u, \qquad B = \frac{\partial u}{\partial x_1} \quad \text{and} \quad C = \frac{\partial u}{\partial x_2}$$

equation (5.1) can be written as three first-order equations

$$e_1 = \frac{\partial B}{\partial x_1} + \frac{\partial C}{\partial x_2} - RAB = 0 \tag{5.1a}$$

$$e_2 = B - \frac{\partial A}{\partial x_1} = 0 \tag{5.1b}$$

$$e_3 = C - \frac{\partial A}{\partial x_2} = 0 \tag{5.1c}$$

Since we have three simultaneous equations, the function (5.2) can be written as

$$\min I = \iint_V (e_1^2 w_1 + e_2^2 w_2 + e_3^2 w_3)\, \mathrm{d}V \tag{5.2a}$$

When using finite elements the domain V is covered by a set of grid points P_k and divided into a set of elements V_i having grid points at the intersections.

On each element V_i we define four bilinear shape functions $\phi_{ki}(x)$ for $k = 1, 4$ such that

$$\phi_{ki}(x) = 1 \text{ at } P_k \in V_i$$

$$\phi_{ki}(x) = 0 \text{ at } P_j \text{ for } j \neq k,\ P_j \in V_i \text{ and at all points } x \notin V_i$$

it is then possible to approximate the unknown variables A, B *and* C (of equations (5.1a)–(5.1c)) by linear combinations of these shape functions as follows:

$$A = \sum_k a_k \phi_{ki}(x),\ B = \sum_k b_k \phi_{ki}(x) \text{ and } C = \sum_k c_k \phi_{ki}(x)$$

where $x \in V_i$ and equations (5.1a), (5.1b) and (5.1c) respectively become

$$e_1 = \sum_{k=1}^{4} b_k \frac{\partial \phi_{ki}}{\partial x_1} + \sum_{k=1}^{4} c_k \frac{\partial \phi_{ki}}{\partial x_2} - R \sum_{k=1}^{4} a_k \phi_{ki} \sum_{j=1}^{4} b_j \phi_{ji} = 0 \tag{5.3a}$$

$$e_2 = \sum_{k=1}^{4} b_k \phi_{ki} - \sum_{k=1}^{4} a_k \frac{\partial \phi_{ki}}{\partial x_1} = 0 \tag{5.3b}$$

$$e_3 = \sum_{k=1}^{4} c_k \phi_{ki} - \sum_{k=1}^{4} a_k \frac{\partial \phi_{ki}}{\partial x_2} = 0 \tag{5.3c}$$

The function, gradient and Hessian can now be completely defined and calculated from the available information

$$F = \sum_i \iint_{V_i} (w_1 e_1^2 + w_2 e_2^2 + w_3 e_3^2)\, \mathrm{d}V \tag{5.4}$$

Table 5.1

e_1	e_2	e_3
$\dfrac{\partial e_1}{\partial a_k} = -R\phi_{ki} \sum_{j=1}^{4} b_j\phi_{ji}$	$\dfrac{\partial e_2}{\partial a_k} = -\dfrac{\partial \phi_{ki}}{\partial x_1}$	$\dfrac{\partial e_3}{\partial a_k} = -\dfrac{\partial \phi_{ki}}{\partial x_2}$
$\dfrac{\partial e_1}{\partial b_k} = \dfrac{\partial \phi_{ki}}{\partial x_1} - R\phi_{ki} \sum_{j=1}^{4} a_j\phi_{ji}$	$\dfrac{\partial e_2}{\partial b_k} = \phi_{ki}$	$\dfrac{\partial e_3}{\partial b_k} = 0$
$\dfrac{\partial e_1}{\partial c_k} = \dfrac{\partial \phi_{ki}}{\partial x_2}$	$\dfrac{\partial e_2}{\partial c_k} = 0$	$\dfrac{\partial e_3}{\partial c_k} = \phi_{ki}$

utilising the fact that $e_{i=1,2,3}$ only depends on z_j if $P_j \in V_i$

$$g_j = \frac{\partial F}{\partial z_j} = 2 \sum \iint_{V_i} \left(w_1 e_1 \frac{\partial e_1}{\partial \mathbf{z}_j} + w_2 e_2 \frac{\partial e_2}{\partial \mathbf{z}_j} + w_3 e_3 \frac{\partial e_3}{\partial \mathbf{z}_j} \right) \quad (5.5)$$

where the Jacobian $\partial e_i/\partial \mathbf{z}$ is obtained by differentiating equations (5.3)–(5.3b). If $x \in V_i$, then a typical term $\partial e_i(x)/\partial a_k$ is identically zero if $P_k \notin V_i$. If $P_k \in V_i$, the expressions for the derivatives are given in Table 5.1 where the summation is over the four shape functions relating to V_i.

Forming each g_i and letting $\phi_k = \phi_{ki}$ (drop the element numbering), we shall arrive at the expressions

$$\begin{aligned} g_1 = 2 \sum \iint & - Rw_1\phi_i\left(\sum b_k \frac{\partial \phi_k}{\partial x_1} + \sum c_k \frac{\partial \phi_k}{\partial x_2}\right. \\ & \left. - R \sum a_k\phi_k \sum b_j\phi_j\right) \sum b_k\phi_k \\ & - \left(\sum b_k\phi_k - \sum a_k \frac{\partial \phi_k}{\partial x_1}\right) w_2 \frac{\partial \phi_k}{\partial x_1} \\ & - \left(\sum c_k\phi_k - \sum a_k \frac{\partial \phi_k}{\partial x_2}\right) w_3 \frac{\partial \phi_k}{\partial x_2} \, dV \end{aligned} \quad (5.6a)$$

$$\begin{aligned} g_2 = 2 \sum \iint & w_1 \frac{\partial \phi_i}{\partial x_1} \left(\sum b_k \frac{\partial \phi_k}{\partial x_1} + \sum c_k \frac{\partial \phi_k}{\partial x_2}\right. \\ & \left. - R \sum a_k\phi_k \sum b_j\phi_j\right) \\ & - R\phi_i \left(\sum b_k \frac{\partial \phi_k}{\partial x_1} + \sum c_k \frac{\partial \phi_k}{\partial x_2}\right. \\ & \left. - R \sum a_k\phi_k \sum b_j\phi_j\right) w_1 \sum a_k\phi_k \\ & + \left(\sum b_k\phi_k - \sum a_k \frac{\partial \phi_k}{\partial x_1}\right) w_2\phi_i \, dV \end{aligned} \quad (5.6b)$$

$$g_3 = 2\sum\iint w_1 \frac{\partial\phi_i}{\partial x_2}\left(\sum b_k \frac{\partial\phi_k}{\partial x_1} + \sum c_k \frac{\partial\phi_k}{\partial x_2} - R\sum a_k\phi_k \sum b_j\phi_j\right) + w_3\phi_i\left(\sum c_k\phi_k - \sum a_k \frac{\partial\phi_k}{\partial x_2}\right) \mathrm{d}V \tag{5.6c}$$

and the Hessian $\nabla^2 I$ $(=G)$ will be given by

$$\nabla^2 I^{\mathrm{el}}_{ij} = 2\iint_{V_i} \frac{\partial g_{ki}}{\partial z_{lj}} \mathrm{d}V \tag{5.7}$$

for all $i, j = 1, 4$ and all $k, l = 1, 3$ (where g_{ki} denotes the kth entry of g at node i and z_{lj} denotes the lth unknown at node j; also the vector **g** has been obtained from equation (5.5) and is expressed as equations (5.8). The element matrices are 12×12 in size (three unknowns and four nodes) and are arranged in groups of 3×3 blocks; they are also block symmetric, as follows.

$i \backslash j$	node 1			node 2			node 3			node 4		
node 1	$\frac{\partial g_1}{\partial a}$	$\frac{\partial g_1}{\partial b}$	$\frac{\partial g_1}{\partial c}$									
	$\frac{\partial g_2}{\partial a}$	$\frac{\partial g_2}{\partial b}$	$\frac{\partial g_2}{\partial c}$									
	$\frac{\partial g_3}{\partial a}$	$\frac{\partial g_3}{\partial b}$	$\frac{\partial g_3}{\partial c}$									
node 2												
node 3												
node 4										$\frac{\partial g_1}{\partial a}$	$\frac{\partial g_1}{\partial b}$	$\frac{\partial g_1}{\partial c}$
										$\frac{\partial g_2}{\partial a}$	$\frac{\partial g_2}{\partial b}$	$\frac{\partial g_2}{\partial c}$
										$\frac{\partial g_3}{\partial a}$	$\frac{\partial g_3}{\partial b}$	$\frac{\partial g_3}{\partial c}$

To obtain the 3 × 3 block of equations we differentiate equations (5.6a)–(5.6c) with respect to each of the three unknowns a, b and c. This results in the following expressions where ϕ_i, ϕ_j relate directly to nodes i and j for the current element:

$$\frac{\partial g_1}{\partial a} = R^2 w_1 \phi_i \phi_j (\sum b_k \phi_k)^2 + w_2 \frac{\partial \phi_i}{\partial x_1} \frac{\partial \phi_j}{\partial x_1} + w_3 \frac{\partial \phi_i}{\partial x_2} \frac{\partial \phi_j}{\partial x_2}$$

$$\frac{\partial g_1}{\partial b} = - R w_1 \phi_i \Big\{ \phi_j \Big[\sum b_k \frac{\partial \phi_k}{\partial x_1} + \sum c_k \frac{\partial \phi_k}{\partial x_2}$$

$$- (R \sum a_k \phi_k)(2 \sum b_j \phi_j \Big] + \sum b_k \phi_k \frac{\partial \phi_j}{\partial x_1} \Big\} - w_2 \frac{\partial \phi_i}{\partial x_1} \phi_j$$

$$\frac{\partial g_1}{\partial c} = -R w_1 \phi_i (\sum b_k \phi_k) \frac{\partial \phi_j}{\partial x_2} - w_3 \frac{\partial \phi_i}{\partial x_2} \phi_j$$

$$\frac{\partial g_2}{\partial a} = -R w_1 \Big[\frac{\partial \phi_i}{\partial x_1} (\sum b_k \phi_k) \phi_j + \phi_i \phi_j \Big(\sum b_k \frac{\partial \phi_k}{\partial x_1} + \sum c_k \frac{\partial \phi_k}{\partial x_2}$$

$$- 2R \sum b_k \phi_k \sum a_j \phi_j \Big) \Big] - w_2 \phi_i \frac{\partial \phi_j}{\partial x_1}$$

$$\frac{\partial g_2}{\partial b} = w_1 \frac{\partial \phi_i}{\partial x_1} \Big(\frac{\partial \phi_j}{\partial x_1} - R \phi_j \sum a_k \phi_k \Big) - R \phi_i w_1 \sum a_k \phi_k \Big(\frac{\partial \phi_j}{\partial x_1}$$

$$- R \phi_j \sum a_k \phi_k \Big) + w_2 \phi_i \phi_j \tag{5.8}$$

$$\frac{\partial g_2}{\partial c} = w_1 \frac{\partial \phi_i}{\partial x_1} \frac{\partial \phi_j}{\partial x_2} - R w_1 \phi_i \Big(\sum a_k \phi_k \Big) \frac{\partial \phi_j}{\partial x_2}$$

$$\frac{\partial g_3}{\partial a} = - R w_1 \frac{\partial \phi_i}{\partial x_2} \phi_j \sum b_k \phi_k - w_3 \phi_i \frac{\partial \phi_j}{\partial x_2}$$

$$\frac{\partial g_3}{\partial b} = \frac{w_1 \partial \phi_i}{\partial x_2} \Big(\frac{\partial \phi_j}{\partial x_1} - R \phi_j \sum a_k \phi_k \Big)$$

$$\frac{\partial g_3}{\partial c} = w_1 \frac{\partial \phi_i}{\partial x_2} \frac{\partial \phi_j}{\partial x_2} + w_3 \phi_i \phi_j$$

Each of these equations now have to be integrated over the element. This is achieved using Gaussian quadrature with a 3 × 3 set of quadrature points. An alternative approach is described in section 5.2.2.

5.2.2 Solution by least squares: formulation II

In section 5.2.1, products of the following form were evaluated:

$$\iint_V \sum a_k \frac{\partial \phi_k}{\partial x_1} \, dV \tag{5.9}$$

This expression can be rearranged to give

$$\sum a_k \iint_V \frac{\partial \phi_k}{\partial x_1} \, \mathrm{d}V \tag{5.10}$$

Now, since our mesh and set of shape functions are fixed, it is unnecessary to recalculate the integral every time that we require f, $\mathbf{g}$ or G. By initially calculating all the integrals required and storing them, it is possible subsequently to index into store to obtain the values required for f, $\mathbf{g}$ and G.

By writing out equation (5.2a) in full, we arrive at

$$\begin{aligned} I = \iint \Bigg\{ & \left(\sum b_j \frac{\partial \phi_j}{\partial x_1} + \sum c_j \frac{\partial \phi_j}{\partial x_2} - R \sum a_j \phi_j \sum b_k \phi_k \right)^2 w_1 \\ & + \left(\sum b_j \phi_j - \sum a_j \frac{\partial \phi_j}{\partial x_1} \right)^2 w_2 \\ & + \left(\sum c_k \phi_k - \sum a_j \frac{\partial \phi_j}{\partial x_2} \right)^2 w_3 \Bigg\} \, \mathrm{d}V \end{aligned} \tag{5.11}$$

and by expanding and separating the integrals we get

$$\begin{aligned} I = \sum_{\mathrm{el}} \Bigg(& \sum\sum b_{j1} b_{j2} \iint \frac{\partial \phi_{j1}}{\partial x_1} \frac{\partial \phi_{j2}}{\partial x_1} + 2 \sum\sum b_i c_j \iint \frac{\partial \phi_i}{\partial x_1} \frac{\partial \phi_j}{\partial x_2} \\ & - 2R \sum\sum\sum b_i a_j c_k \iint \frac{\partial \phi_i}{\partial x_1} \phi_j \phi_k \\ & + \sum\sum c_{j1} c_{j2} \iint \frac{\partial \phi_{j1}}{\partial x_2} \frac{\partial \phi_{j2}}{\partial x_2} - 2R \sum\sum\sum c_i a_j c_k \iint \frac{\partial \phi_i}{\partial x_2} \phi_j \phi_k \\ & + R^2 \sum\sum\sum\sum a_{j1} a_{j2} b_{k1} b_{k2} \iint \phi_{j1} \phi_{j2} \phi_{k1} \phi_{k2} \Bigg) w_1 \\ & + \left(\sum\sum b_{j1} b_{j2} \iint \phi_{j1} \phi_{j2} - 2 \sum\sum a_i b_j \iint \frac{\partial \phi_i}{\partial x_1} \phi_j \right. \\ & \left. + \sum\sum a_{j1} a_{j2} \iint \frac{\partial \phi_{j1}}{\partial x_1} \frac{\partial \phi_{j2}}{\partial x_2} \right) w_2 \\ & + \left(\sum\sum c_{j1} c_{j2} \iint \phi_{j1} \phi_{j2} - 2 \sum\sum c_i a_j \iint \phi_i \frac{\partial \phi_j}{\partial x_2} \right. \\ & \left. + \sum\sum a_{j1} a_{j2} \iint \frac{\partial \phi_{j1}}{\partial x_2} \frac{\partial \phi_{j2}}{\partial x_2} \right) w_3 \end{aligned} \tag{5.12}$$

Differentiating (5.12) with respect to the three unknowns a, b and c, we arrive at the three following expressions for the gradient at each node:

$$g_1 = \frac{\partial I}{\partial a_m} = \left[-2R \sum\sum b_i b_k \iint \frac{\partial \phi_i}{\partial x_1} \phi_m \phi_k \right.$$

$$- 2R \sum c_i b_k \iint \frac{\partial \phi_i}{\partial x_2} \phi_m \phi_k$$

$$+ R^2 \sum\sum\sum a_j b_1 b_{k2} \left(\iint \phi_m \phi_j \phi_{k1} \phi_{k2} \right.$$

$$\left.\left. + \iint \phi_j \phi_m \phi_{k1} \phi_{k2} \right) \right] w_1$$

$$\left[- 2 \sum b_i \iint \frac{\partial \phi_m}{\partial x_1} \phi_j - \sum a_j \left(\iint \frac{\partial \phi_m}{\partial x_1} \frac{\partial \phi_j}{\partial x_1} \right.\right.$$

$$\left.\left. + \iint \frac{\partial \phi_j}{\partial x_1} \frac{\partial \phi_m}{\partial x_1} \right) \right] w_2$$

$$\left[- 2 \sum c_i \iint \phi_i \quad \frac{\partial \phi_m}{\partial x_2} + \sum a_j \left(\iint \frac{\partial \phi_j}{\partial x_2} \frac{\partial \phi_m}{\partial x_2} \right.\right.$$

$$\left.\left. + \iint \frac{\partial \phi_m}{\partial x_2} \frac{\partial \phi_j}{\partial x_2} \right) \right] w_3 \tag{5.13a}$$

$$g_2 = \frac{\partial I}{\partial b_m} = \left[\sum b_j \left(\iint \frac{\partial \phi_m}{\partial x_1} \frac{\partial \phi_j}{\partial x_1} + \iint \frac{\partial \phi_j}{\partial x_1} \frac{\partial \phi_m}{\partial x_1} \right) \right.$$

$$+ 2 \sum c_j \iint \frac{\partial \phi_m}{\partial x_1} \frac{\partial \phi_j}{\partial x_2}$$

$$- 2R \sum\sum b_i a_j \left(\iint \phi_j \phi_i \frac{\partial \phi_m}{\partial x_1} + \iint \frac{\partial \phi_i}{\partial x_1} \phi_j \phi_m \right)$$

$$- 2R \sum\sum c_i a_j \iint \frac{\partial \phi_i}{\partial x_2} \phi_j \phi_m$$

$$+ R^2 \sum\sum\sum a_{j1} a_{j2} b_k \left(\iint \phi_{j1} \phi_{j2} \phi_m \phi_k \right.$$

$$\left.\left. + \iint \phi_{j1} \phi_{j2} \phi_k \phi_m \right) \right] w_1$$

$$+ \left[\sum b_j \left(\iint \phi_m \phi_j + \iint \phi_j \phi_m \right) \right.$$

$$\left. - 2 \sum a_i \iint \frac{\partial \phi_i}{\partial x_1} \phi_m \right] w_2 \tag{5.13b}$$

$$g_3 = \frac{\partial I}{\partial c_m} = \left[2\sum b_i \iint \frac{\partial \phi_i}{\partial x_2}\frac{\partial \phi_m}{\partial x_2} + \sum c_j\left(\iint \frac{\partial \phi_m}{\partial x_2}\frac{\partial \phi_i}{\partial x_2}\right.\right.$$

$$\left.\left. + \iint \frac{\partial \phi_j}{\partial x_2}\frac{\partial \phi_m}{\partial x_2}\right) - 2R\sum\sum a_j b_k \iint \frac{\partial \phi_m}{\partial x_2}\phi_j\phi_k\right] w_1$$

$$+ \left[\sum c_j\left(\iint \phi_m\phi_j + \iint \phi_j\phi_m\right)\right.$$

$$\left. - 2\sum a_j \iint \phi_m \frac{\partial \phi_j}{\partial x_2}\right] w_3 \qquad (5.13c)$$

These equations can be abbreviated by realising that

$$\sum a_j\left(\iint \frac{\partial \phi_m}{\partial x_1}\frac{\partial \phi_j}{\partial x_1} + \iint \frac{\partial \phi_j}{\partial x_1}\frac{\partial \phi_m}{\partial x_1}\right) = 2\sum a_j \iint \frac{\partial \phi_m}{\partial x_1}\frac{\partial \phi_j}{\partial x_1} \qquad (5.14a)$$

$$\sum b_j\left(\iint \phi_m\phi_j + \iint \phi_j\phi_m\right) = 2\sum b_j \iint \phi_m\phi_j \qquad (5.14b)$$

$$\sum\sum\sum a_{j1}a_{j2}b_k\left(\iint \phi_{j1}\phi_{j2}\phi_k\phi_m + \iint \phi_{j1}\phi_{j2}\phi_m\phi_k\right) =$$

$$2\sum\sum\sum a_{j1}a_{j2}b_k \iint \phi_{j1}\phi_{j2}\phi_m\phi_k \qquad 5.14c)$$

but

$$\sum b_i a_j\left(\iint \frac{\partial \phi_m}{\partial x_1}\phi_i\phi_j + \iint \frac{\partial \phi_i}{\partial x_1}\phi_j\phi_m\right) \neq 2\sum b_i a_j \iint \frac{\partial \phi_m}{\partial x_1}\phi_i\phi_j \qquad (5.15)$$

Hence by substituting (14a)–(14c) into equations (13a)–(13c) and differentiating each of the new equations with respect to the three unknowns a, b and c, we obtain the 3×3 blocks of our Hessian G (which has the same structure as in section 5.2.1).

The new equation becomes

$$\frac{\partial g_1}{\partial a_{n,m}} = 2R^2 w_1 \sum\sum b_{k1}b_{k2}\iint \phi_m\phi_n\phi_{k1}\phi_{k2}$$

$$+ 2w_2 \iint \frac{\partial \phi_m}{\partial x_1}\frac{\partial \phi_n}{\partial x_1} + 2w_3 \iint \frac{\partial \phi_m}{\partial x_2}\frac{\partial \phi_n}{\partial x_2}$$

$$\frac{\partial g_1}{\partial b_{n,m}} = -2\left\{Rw_1\left[\sum b_i\left(\iint \frac{\partial \phi_n}{\partial x_1}\phi_i\phi_m\right.\right.\right.$$

$$\left. + \iint \frac{\partial \phi_i}{\partial x_1}\phi_n\phi_m\right) + \sum c_i \iint \frac{\partial \phi_i}{\partial x_2}\phi_n\phi_m$$

$$\left. -2R\sum\sum a_j b_k \iint \phi_n\phi_j\phi_k\phi_m\right] + w_2 \iint \frac{\partial \phi_m}{\partial x_1}\phi_n$$

$$\frac{\partial g_1}{\partial c_{n,m}} = -2\left(Rw_1 \sum b_k \iint \frac{\partial \phi_n}{\partial x_2} \phi_k \phi_m + w_3 \iint \frac{\partial \phi_m}{\partial x_2} \phi_n\right)$$

$$\begin{aligned}\frac{\partial g_2}{\partial a_{n,m}} = -2\Bigg\{Rw_1\Bigg[\sum b_i \Bigg(\iint \frac{\partial \phi_m}{\partial x_1} \phi_n \phi_i \\ + \iint \frac{\partial \phi_i}{\partial x_1} \phi_n \phi_m\Bigg) + \sum c_i \iint \frac{\partial \phi_i}{\partial x_2} \phi_n \phi_m \\ -2R \sum\sum a_j b_k \iint \phi_n \phi_j \phi_m \phi_k\Bigg] + w_2 \iint \frac{\partial \phi_n}{\partial x_1} \phi_m\Bigg\}\end{aligned} \tag{5.16}$$

$$\begin{aligned}\frac{\partial g_2}{\partial b_{n,m}} = 2\Bigg\{W_1\Bigg[\iint \frac{\partial \phi_m}{\partial x_1} \frac{\partial \phi_n}{\partial x_1} \\ - R \sum a_j \left(\iint \phi_j \phi_n \frac{\partial \phi_m}{\partial x_1} + \iint \frac{\partial \phi_n}{\partial x_1} \phi_j \phi_m\right) \\ + R^2 \sum\sum a_{j1} a_{j2} \iint \phi_{j2} \phi_m \phi_n\Bigg] + w_2 \iint \phi_m \phi_n\Bigg\}\end{aligned}$$

$$\frac{\partial g_2}{\partial c_{n,m}} = 2w_1\left(\iint \frac{\partial \phi_m}{\partial x_1} \frac{\partial \phi_n}{\partial x_2} - R \sum a_j \iint \frac{\partial \phi_n}{\partial x_2} \phi_j \phi_m\right)$$

$$\frac{\partial g_3}{\partial a_{n,m}} = -2\left(Rw_1 \sum b_k \iint \frac{\partial \phi_m}{\partial x_2} \phi_n \phi_k + w_3 \iint \frac{\partial \phi_n}{\partial x_2} \phi_m\right)$$

$$\frac{\partial g_3}{\partial b_{n,m}} = 2w_1\left(\iint \frac{\partial \phi_n}{\partial x_1} \frac{\partial \phi_m}{\partial x_2} - R \sum a_j \iint \frac{\partial \phi_m}{\partial x_2} \phi_j \phi_n\right)$$

$$\frac{\partial g_3}{\partial c_{n,m}} = 2\left(w_1 \iint \frac{\partial \phi_m}{\partial x_2} \frac{\partial \phi_n}{\partial x_2} + w_3 \iint \phi_m \phi_n\right)$$

Having now obtained expressions for f, $\mathbf{g}$ and G, it is necessary only to store the following integrals:

Integral	Combinations	Unique values	
$\iint \phi_i \phi_j \, dV$	16	3	(5.17a)
$\iint \frac{\partial \phi_i}{\partial x_1} \phi_j \, dV$	16	4	(5.17b)
$\iint \frac{\partial \phi_i}{\partial x_2} \phi_j \, dV$	16	4	(5.17c)
$\iint \frac{\partial \phi_i}{\partial x_1} \frac{\partial \phi_j}{\partial x_1} \, dV$	16	4	(5.17d)

Integral	Combinations	Unique values	
$\iint \frac{\partial\phi_i}{\partial x_2}\frac{\partial\phi_j}{\partial x_2}\,dV$	16	4	(5.17e)
$\iint \frac{\partial\phi_i}{\partial x_1}\frac{\partial\phi_j}{\partial x_2}\,dV$	16	2	(5.17f)
$\iint \frac{\partial\phi_i}{\partial x_1}\phi_j\phi_k\,dV$	64	8	(5.17g)
$\iint \frac{\partial\phi_i}{\partial x_2}\phi_j\phi_k\,dV$	64	8	(5.17h)
$\iint \phi_i\phi_j\phi_k\phi_l\,dV$	256	6	(5.17i)
Total storage	480	43	

The total storage required can be seen to be 15,360 planes (480 × 32 bits). Taking this together with existing storage requirements would far exceed our available 16K planes. Fortunately, however, not all these values are unique as is indicated above; the actual unique integrals can be stored in 1,376 planes (43 × 32) bits). Therefore, all that is now required for the implementation is an indexing vector to be set up for each of the integrals, allowing us access to the correct integral for a given set of subscripts $(i, j, \ldots)$.

In sections 5.3 and sections 5.4 we shall describe the conjugate gradient approach and the truncated Newton approach respectively for completing the solution of the problem.

5.3 NON-LINEAR CONJUGATE GRADIENTS

The non-linear conjugate gradient algorithm that was used was based on the Fletcher and Reeves [1] proposals and is described as follows.

(1) Select an initial estimate for $\mathbf{x}^{(0)}$ where $k = 0$.
(2) Perform initialisation for the line search.
(3) Calculate $f^{(k)} = f(\mathbf{x}^{(k)})$.
(4) Calculate $\mathbf{g}^{(k)} = g(\mathbf{x}^{(k)})$.
(5) Evaluate $\mathbf{g}^{(k)\mathrm{T}} \cdot \mathbf{g}^{(k)}$.
(6) If either $\mathbf{g}^{(k)\mathrm{T}} \cdot \mathbf{g}^{(k)} < e_0$ or k is greater than the maximum number of iterations, then *stop*..
(7) If this is the first iteration, the set direction $\mathbf{p}^{(k)} = -\mathbf{g}^{(k)}$, or else set

$$\beta^{(k)} = \frac{\mathbf{g}^{(k)\mathrm{T}} \cdot \mathbf{g}^{(k)}}{\mathbf{g}^{(k-1)\mathrm{T}} \cdot \mathbf{g}^{(k-1)}}$$

and then update the direction such that

$$\mathbf{p}^{(k)} = -\mathbf{g}^{(k)} + \beta^{(k)}\mathbf{p}^{(k-1)}.$$

(8) Perform scaling of the step length $\alpha^{(k)}$ prior to the line search.
(9) Call a suitable line search routine.
(10) Set $\mathbf{x}^{(k+1)} = \mathbf{x}^{(k)} + \alpha^{(k)}\mathbf{p}^{(k)}$.
(11) Set $k = k + 1$.
(12) Go to step (4).

5.4 TRUNCATED NEWTON APPROACH

This approach is an alternative to the non-linear conjugate gradient approach. In this method we are in effect solving a series of linear problems (step (4)) by utilising a linear conjugate gradient algorithm. The Newton method is described as follows.

(1) Initialise $\mathbf{x}^{(0)}$, set $k = 0$ and calculate $f(\mathbf{x}^{(k)})$.
(2) Calculate $g(\mathbf{x}^{(k)})$ and $G(\mathbf{x}^{(k)})$.
(3) If $\mathbf{g}^{(k)\mathrm{T}} \cdot \mathbf{g}^{(k)} < e_0$ or $k > k_{\max}$, then *stop*.
(4) Solve the problem $A\mathbf{u} = -\mathbf{g}$ where $A = G(\mathbf{x}^{(k)})$.
(5) Check the following. If $\mathbf{u}$ satisfies Wolfe's condition 1 (namely $-\mathbf{u}^{\mathrm{T}} \cdot \mathbf{g} > e_1 \|u\| \|g\|$), then go to step (6) or else go to step (7).
(6) Set $\mathbf{p} = \mathbf{u}$, $\alpha = 1$ and check the following. If $f(\mathbf{x}^{(k)} + \alpha\mathbf{u})$ satisfies Wolfe's conditions II and III (namely $|f(\mathbf{x}^{(k)}) + \mathbf{g}^{\mathrm{T}} \cdot \mathbf{p} - f(\mathbf{x}^{(k+1)})| > e_2\mathbf{g}^{\mathrm{T}} \cdot \mathbf{p}$ and $f(\mathbf{x}^{(k)}) - f(\mathbf{x}^{(k+1)}) > -e_3\mathbf{p}^{\mathrm{T}} \cdot \mathbf{g}$), then set $\mathbf{x}^{(k+1)} = \mathbf{x}^{(k)} + \alpha^{(k)}\mathbf{u}$, $k = k + 1$ and go to step (2), or else call a line search to find a value of α that does satisfy Wolfe's conditions II and III, then update $\mathbf{x}$, k and go to step (2).
(7) Replace A by an appropriate positive definite matrix and go to step (4).

Suitable choices for e_0, e_1, e_2 and e_3 would be $1e - 10$, 0.001, 0.1 and 0.0001 respectively.

This method posesses fast second-order convergence provided that the matrix A is not too ill conditioned at step (5). At step (4) where the system of equations $A\mathbf{u} = -\mathbf{g}$ is solved, the following linear conjugate gradient algorithm is used.

(1) Set $\mathbf{r}^{0)} = -\mathbf{g}^{(0)}$, $\mathbf{d}^{(0)} = \mathbf{r}^{(0)}$, $\mathbf{u}^{(0)} = 0$ and $j = 0$.
(2) Set the step length α such that

$$\alpha^{(j)} = \frac{\mathbf{r}^{(j)\mathrm{T}} \cdot \mathbf{r}^{(j)}}{\mathbf{d}^{(j)\mathrm{T}} \cdot A\mathbf{d}^{(j)}}$$

(3) Update the unknown **u** and residual **r**:

$$\mathbf{u}^{(j+1)} = \mathbf{u}^{(j)} + \alpha^{(j)}\mathbf{d}^{(j)}$$

$$\mathbf{r}^{(j+1)} = \mathbf{r}^{(j)} - \alpha^{(j)}A\mathbf{d}^{(j)}$$

(4) If $\| \mathbf{r}^{(j+1)} \| / \| / \mathbf{g} \| < e_4$ or $j > j_{\max}$, then *stop*.

(5) Set

$$\beta^{(j)} = \frac{\mathbf{r}^{(j+1)\mathrm{T}} \cdot \mathbf{r}^{(j+1)}}{\mathbf{r}^{(j)\mathrm{T}} \cdot \mathbf{r}^{(j)}}$$

and update the direction **d**:

$$\mathbf{d}^{(j+1)} = \mathbf{r}^{(j+1)} + \beta^{(j)}\mathbf{d}^{(j)}$$

$$j = j + 1$$

(6) Go to step (2).

A suitable value for e_4 was taken to be $1e - 3$.

5.5 LINE SEARCH

The line search used is a relaxed line search; if the function $I(\alpha)$ is denoted by

$$I(\alpha) = f(\mathrm{x} + \alpha\,\mathrm{d})$$

where x is the initial point and d is a direction, then we require to find the point α which effectively reduces the function $I(\alpha)$ by a quantity bounded away from zero. The line search makes use of parabolic interpolation by initially fitting a parabola and predicting the position of the minimum. If this predicted point satisfies Wolfe's conditions II and III as it always will do for quadratic functions, the search is terminated; otherwise the Armijo [2] method is introduced where we successively halve or double the initial step size until a satisfactory point is obtained.

In section 5.6 we shall examine a form of preconditioning to the system of equations $A\mathrm{u} = -\mathrm{g}$ and see how this can improve the convergence.

5.6 PRECONDITIONING

There have been numerous preconditioning methods proposed for sequential computers; however, when moving an algorithm from a sequential to a parallel architecture, we may experience considerable difficulties. This was demonstrated in some of the work that was done on global optimisation (Appendix 1).

Therefore it was decided simply to improve convergence by scaling the linear system of equations and not to attempt either to use known more complex preconditioners, which did not readily map onto the parallelism of the DAP, or to devise an appropriate method for the DAP.

The approach that we chose was that given by Forsythe and Moler [3]; it was included by Kightley and Jones [4] in their test of the effect of various preconditioners when used on the CRAY-1 and was usually faster (in time but not iterations) in the results which they presented.

It is as follows. The system of equations is given by

$$A\mathbf{u} = \mathbf{f} \tag{5.18}$$

This is the system to be solved inside our linear conjugate gradient code described previously at the end of section 5.4.

The system (5.18) will be scaled by matrices D_1 and D_2 such that

$$\mathbf{u} = D_1\hat{\mathbf{u}} \text{ and } \mathbf{f} = D_2\hat{\mathbf{f}}$$

$$A(D_1\hat{\mathbf{u}}) = D_2\hat{\mathbf{f}} \tag{5.19a}$$

or

$$D_2^{-1}AD_1\hat{\mathbf{u}} = \hat{\mathbf{f}} \tag{5.19b}$$

giving a new linear system with $\hat{A} = D_2^{-1}AD_1 \cdot \hat{A}$ is said to be diagonally equivalent to A if non-singular diagonal matrices D_1 and D_2 exist. The ideal choice for D_1, D_2 would be one which reduced the condition number of $\hat{A}$, producing an improved eigenstructure. However, choosing an optimal D_1 and D_2 proves difficult; our choice was

$$D_1^{\mathrm{T}} = D_2^{-1}$$

where

$$(D_1)_{ij} = \begin{cases} A_{ij}^{-1/2}, & i = j \\ 0, & i \neq j \end{cases}$$

which gives

$$\hat{a}_{ij} = \frac{a_{ij}}{\sqrt{(a_{ii}a_{jj})}} \tag{5.20}$$

where A is now scaled such that $\hat{a}_{ij} = 1$ if $i = j$. This implies that the variable u is scaled so that

$$\hat{u}_i = u_i\sqrt{a_{ii}} \tag{5.21}$$

and the right-hand side f is scaled by

$$\hat{f}_i = \frac{f}{\sqrt{a_{ii}}} \tag{5.22}$$

The important point to remember is that in our system (5.18) *the matrix A is not assembled*; we have element information only. Our system is actually held as

$$A^e\mathbf{u}^e = \mathbf{f}^e \tag{5.23}$$

where each of the A^e matrices is symmetric. This does not pose any significant problems, however, as we can perform our scaling on an element-by-element basis as follows.

The contributions required to form a value a_{ii} come only from elements which have a connection with global node i; hence

$$a_{ii} = \sum_{e=1}^{4} a^e_{L(i),L(i)} \tag{5.24}$$

where $L(i)$ is a function converting global node i into a local node for that particular element e, the summation being performed over the four element matrices local to node i. Once the global set of a_{ii} values has been formed the scaling described in (5.20) becomes

$$\hat{a}_{ij} = \frac{a_{ij}}{\sqrt{(a_{G(i),G(i)}a_{G(j),G(j)})}} \tag{5.25}$$

where $G(i)$ (the inverse of $L(i)$) is a function converting a local node i into a global node (one of the values of the set which was formed at (5.24). The scaling for $\mathbf{u}$ and $\mathbf{f}$ remains as

$$\hat{u}_i = u_i\sqrt{a_{ii}} \tag{5.26}$$

$$\hat{f}_i = \frac{f}{\sqrt{a_{ii}}} \tag{5.27}$$

since both the vectors $\mathbf{u}$ and $\mathbf{f}$ are fully assembled and $\mathbf{u}^e, \mathbf{f}^e$ are simply obtained as subsets if and when required.

When termination is satisfied inside the linear solver, we must rescale the system of equations to get back to the original problem. In fact, since the current matrix A is not used again and the vector $\mathbf{f}$

was preserved on entry, we only need to rescale the vector **u** such that

$$u_i = \frac{\hat{u}_i}{\sqrt{a_{ii}}} \tag{5.28}$$

Full details of how these calculations and others are actually achieved on the DAP are given in Appendix 3.

After describing the region and boundary conditions, the results obtained for both of the formulations, the algorithms and the effect of diagonal scaling will be examined.

5.7 BOUNDARY CONDITIONS

The problem was solved over the square domain (4.0, 4.0) to (4.5, 4.5) with the boundaries being fixed at their true solution

$$A = u = \frac{6x_1}{Rx_2^2}, \qquad B = u_{x1} = \frac{6}{Rx_2^2}, \qquad C = u_{x2} = \frac{-12x_1}{Rx_2^3}$$

5.8 RESULTS

In previous sections in this chapter, two formulations and two algorithms have been described. Before looking at the results, we can make several assumptions about them. Firstly, we would expect formulation II to be faster than formulation I because we are not recalculating the integrals at every iteration. Secondly, we would expect the Newton algorithm to be faster than the non-linear conjugate gradient algorithm because of its fast second- order convergence. Thirdly, we would expect the preconditioned linearised version to improve on the non-preconditioned version. Finally we would naturally expect the DAP to be faster than the sequential machine.

We should note that the overall solution time is the time taken to set up the system plus the number of iterations multiplied by the time per iteration; any values quoted refer to the overall solution time.

The test series commenced with a comparatively small mesh of 5 × 5 and varied the Reynolds number R from 5000 to 5, this being illustrated in Graph 5.1 and Table 5.2 (compare also the corresponding sequential results obtained on a DEC 1091). In Graph 5.1 it is evident that, the smaller the value of R, the more difficult the problem; this also illustrates the point that, as the problem gets more difficult, the two Newton versions L-I and L-II do in fact show a

Table 5.2 Grid size of 5 × 5 (h = 0.125) for the ICL DAP.

	Error			Function value	Iterations	CPU time (s)
	U	UX1	UX2			
R = 5000						
L-I	8.14916E-8	4.35760E-6	6.40751E-6	5.8963E-12	2	8.01
L-II	8.24222E-8	4.32281E-6	6.21252E-6	6.2493E-12	2	6.92
NL-I	2.0188E-6	6.1439E-6	1.286E-5	4.8281E-11	4	5.89
NL-II	2.0327E-6	6.1447E-6	1.2861E-5	4.8514E-11	4	11.59
R = 500						
L-I	5.26197E-8	3.06989E-5	6.4344E-5	3.3093E-10	3	16.27
L-II	9.3132E-9	2.9868E-5	6.4599E-5	3.3829E-10	3	14.02
NL-I	3.9339E-6	5.945E-5	1.2647E-4	1.8364E-9	6	6.37
NL-II	3.9315E-6	5.9468E-5	1.2648E-4	1.8394E-9	6	15.86
R = 250						
L-I	9.6857E-8	6.1425E-5	1.2867E-4	1.32364E-9	3	16.25
L-II	1.1175E-8	5.9769E-8	1.2921E-4	1.4287E-9	3	14.05
Nl-I	2.1942E-6	7.5616E-6	4.2027E-5	1.17213E-9	12	9.6
Nl-II	2.1326E-6	6.9537E-6	4.1815E-5	1.22889E-9	12	32.95

$R = 50$						
L-I	6.92904E-7	3.0858E-4	6.4345E-4	3.2976E-8	4	23.31
L-II	5.6996E-7	3.03607E-4	6.4078E-4	3.4078E-4	4	20.74
NL-I	1.34112E-6	6.4561E-6	5.4531E-6	1.3353E-8	35	33.75
$R = 25$						
L-I	1.3895E-6	6.1714E-4	1.2814E-3	1.31896E-7	4	23.62
L-II	1.28151E-6	6.081E-4	1.2798E-3	1.3526E-7	4	21.76
Nl-I	1.6056E-6	9.8448E-5	7.55931E-5	4.8279E-7	43	44.11
$R = 5$						
L-I	6.91414E-6	3.0859E-3	6.4345E-3	3.2975E-6	4	23.39
L-II	5.3644E-6	3.0409E-3	6.4048E-3	3.3602E-6	4	21.81
NL-I	1.7881E-7	8.8752E-5	5.37812E-4	1.8399E-6	63	68.61

In this and subsequent tables, L-I denotes the (Newton) linearised formulation I, L-II denotes the (Newton) linearised formulation II, NL-I denotes the non-linear conjugate gradient formulation I, NL-II denotes the non-linear conjugate gradient formulation II, U denotes the u value, UX1 denotes the u_{x1} value, UX2 denotes the u_{x2} value, the iterations are the number of non-linear iterations and CPU means central processing unit. All sequential runs were on a DEC 1091 (approximately three times slower than the ICL 2980 which is installed at Queen Mary College).

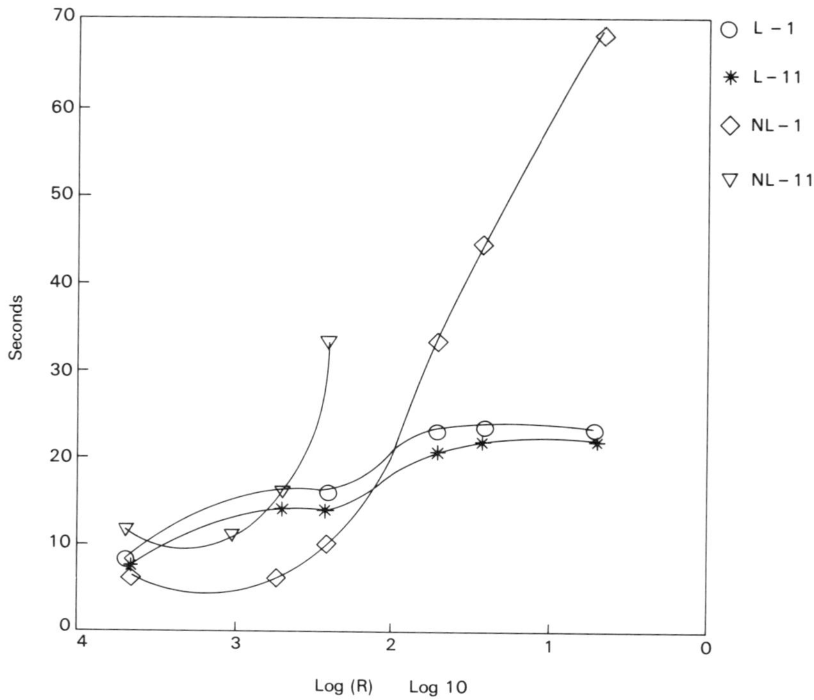

Graph 5.1 Grid size of 5 × 5 (h = 0.125) for the ICL DAP (Table 5.2).

considerable time advantage over the non-linear conjugate gradient versions NL-I and NL-II. In addition to this point L-II shows a slight advantage over L-I. As predicted, this time advantage from Table 5.4 is about 1.18 which is confirmed by the results in Tables 5.2 and 5.5. However, for the non-linear conjugate gradient algorithm the reverse is true. This apparent discrepancy can be explained by again looking at the values and explanation in Table 5.4 and noting the point that in the non-linear conjugate gradient algorithm we only make use of CALFUN (CALculate the FUNction) and CALGRD (CALculate the GRaDient); therefore we would expect the time for NL-II to be at least twice that of NL-1.

Upon studying this graph it became apparent that the two algorithms which we would continue to use would be the linearised formulation II (L-II) and the non-linear conjugate gradient formulation I (NL-I).

The next test case was to take a 9 × 9 grid (Graph 5.2 and Table 5.5) and the difference between NL-I and L-II became even more apparent. The linearised formulation I (L-I) was also plotted on this graph and, as we can see, is separated by almost a constant amount from L-II.

Table 5.3 Grid size of 5 × 5 (h = 0.125) for the DEC 1091

	Error			Function value	Iterations	CPU time (s)
	U	UX1	UX2			
R = 5000						
L-II	8.6383E-8	4.36921E-6	6.2405E-6	6.2227E-12	2	6.29
NL-I	2.01928E-6	6.1439E-6	1.2863E-5	4.5277E-11	4	7.83
R = 500						
L-II	1.45519E-8	3.0598E-5	6.4509E-5	3.3178E-10	3	11.56
NL-I	3.9335E-6	5.9451E-5	1.2647E-4	1.8363E-9	6	9.15
R = 250						
L-II	2.91038E-8	6.11971E-5	1.29018E-4	1.32712E-9	3	12.98
NL-I	2.1801E-6	7.5611E-6	4.2317E-5	1.17192E-9	12	17.15
R = 50						
L-II	6.6799E-7	3.08291E-4	6.4297E-4	3.30628E-8	4	21.42
NL-I	1.31899E-6	6.9925E-6	5.21145E-4	1.33247E-7	35	49.21
R = 25						
L-II	1.33598E-6	6.16582E-4	1.2859E-4	1.3225E-7	4	23.02
NL-I	1.6155E-6	9.8714E-5	7.5593E-5	4.1875E-7	43	63.17
R = 5						
L-II	6.7092E-6	3.0829E-3	6.4295E-3	3.30694E-6	4	22.77
NL-I	4.06057E-7	9.1989E-5	5.3223E-4	1.18415E-6	59	93.02

Table 5.4 Comparative times for calculating function, gradient and element matrices.

	Relative time (s)			
	CALFUN	CALGRD	CALELM	Total
Formulation I	0.259	0.496	1.864	2.619
Formulation II	0.508	0.963	0.748	2.219
Speed-up factor	−2	−2	+2.5	+1.18

The relative speed-up factor is in going from the formulation I to the formulation II. In formulation I we recalculate the integrals every time, whilst in formulation II we *do not*. However, the discrepancy of the extra time required in CALFUN and CALGRD can be explained by all the extra array indexing that is required. The only advantage is in CALculating the ELeMent matrices (CALELM), where most terms have been differentiated out. Hence we would only expect a time advantage for the Newton algorithm where we employ CALELM.

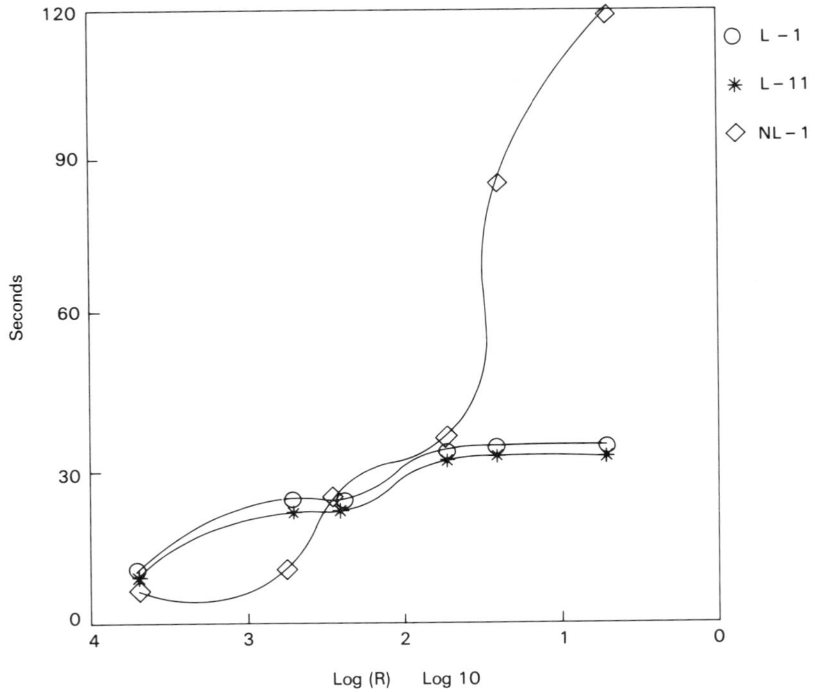

Graph 5.2 Grid size of 9×9 ($h = 0.0625$) for the ICL DAP (Table 5.5).

Table 5.5 Grid size of 9 × 9 (h = 0.0625) for the ICL DAP.

	Error			Function value	Iterations	CPU time (s)
	U	UX1	UX2			
R = 5000						
L-I	8.2175E-8	4.3271E-6	6.3412E-6	5.8861E-12	2	9.96
L-II	2.5378E-8	1.8489E-6	2.3577E-6	9.0994E-12	2	8.82
NL-I	8.4074E-7	6.2672E-6	1.2994E-5	3.4721E-12	6	5.88
R = 500						
L-I	1.3644E-7	1.0475E-5	2.3025E-5	1.0543E-12	3	24.3
L-II	2.50762E-7	5.80493E-6	2.0283E-5	5.9563E-10	3	20.6
NL-I	6.62878E-7	5.9461E-5	1.2758E-4	1.7724E-9	10	10.57
R = 250						
L-I	2.7939E-7	2.0978E-5	4.6041E-5	4.2159E-10	3	24.17
L-II	5.1409E-7	1.1787E-5	4.0571E-5	2.5771E-9	3	21.6
NL-I	1.16603E-6	1.0625E-5	1.2216E-5	4.9859E-10	23	22.87
R = 50						
L-I	1.1027E-6	1.05865E-4	2.3042E-4	1.04443E-8	4	34.21
L-II	1.93345E-6	5.8956E-5	2.0528E-4	5.87345E-8	4	32.0
NL-I	1.3262E-6	2.3856E-5	1.04989E-4	6.69263E-9	37	36.1
R = 25						
l-I	2.2128E-6	2.11719E-4	4.6079E-4	4.1775E-8	4	34.5
L-II	3.8669E-6	1.1882E-4	4.1317E-4	2.3673E-7	4	32.1
NL-I	2.3432E-6	7.6965E-6	4.9025E-6	1.6234E-8	84	82.1
R = 5						
L-I	1.10268E-5	1.05875E-3	2.3042E-3	1.04442E-6	4	34.83
L-II	1.97293E-5	5.9473E-4	2.0682E-3	5.16425E-6	4	32.31
NL-I	1.0132E-6	2.7657E-5	2.1118E-4	3.63541E-7	123	119.5

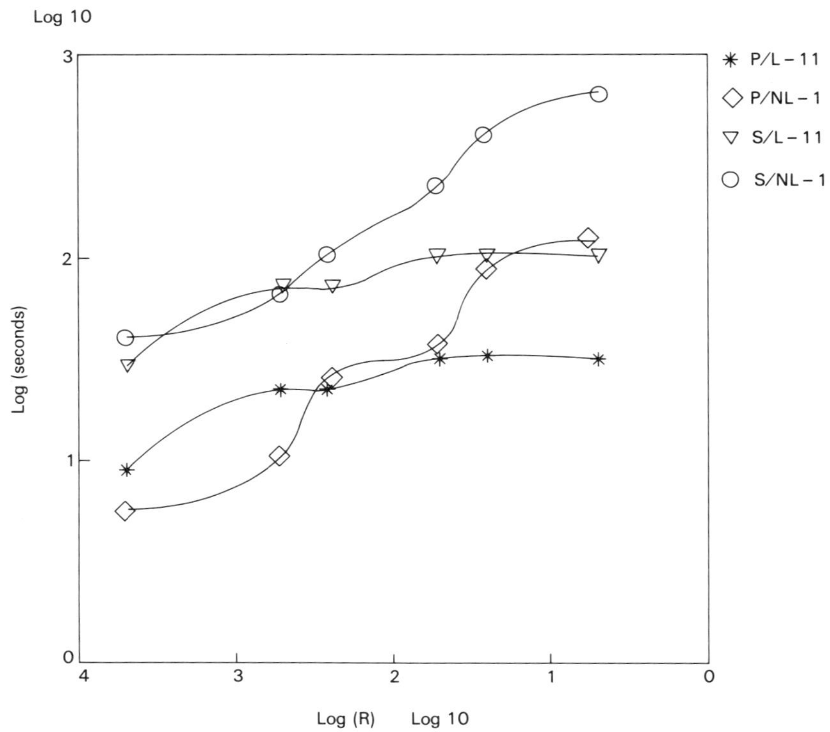

Graph 5.3 Grid size of 9 × 9 (h = 0.0625), comparing L-II and NL-I for parallel runs (denoted P/L-II and P/NL-I) and for sequential runs (denoted S/L-II and S/NL-II) (Tables 5.5 and 5.6).

The third test case was to repeat the second with just the two chosen algorithms, but now comparing them with the same two sequential algorithms (Graph 5.3 and Tables 5.5 and 5.6). Here we see a relative speed-up of approximately 3.2 for the linearised version on the DAP and about 5.2 for the non-linear conjugate gradient version on the DAP. The fact that the non-linear speed-up is more on the DAP can be explained by the fact that the array indexing (of the form A(,,I,J)) in the linearised version on the DAP is expensive. We should also note that this speed-up is at a point where we are still using *only about one-fiftieth of the DAP*.

The next test case was to fix the Reynolds number at 500 and to vary the grid size from 5 × 5 to 63 × 63, this being shown in Graph 5.4 (and Table 5.7 and 5.8). The most striking results here are the sequential runs undertaken. Looking at version NL-I, we see that at a grid size of 39 × 39 (still effectively only three-eighths of the DAP) the sequential computer required in excess of 1 hr to solve

Table 5.6 Grid size of 9×9 ($h = 0.0625$) for the DEC 1091.

	Error			Function value	Iterations	CPU time (s)
	U	UX1	UX2			
$R = 5000$						
L-II	3.68236E-8	2.31881E-6	2.5927E-6	3.2190E-12	2	28.41
NL-I	8.4047E-7	6.2673E-6	1.2994E-5	3.472E-11	6	39.78
$R = 500$						
L-II	1.64902E-7	1.01333E-5	2.2764E-5	1.0765E-10	3	69.39
NL-I	6.61792E-7	5.94612E-5	1.2758E-4	1.7723E-9	10	66.3
$R = 250$						
l-II	3.298E-7	2.02665E-5	4.5528E-5	4.3061E-10	3	69.53
NL-I	1.1651E-6	1.0637E-5	1.2371E-5	5.0137E-10	23	103.2
$R = 50$						
L-II	1.05192E-6	1.05596E-4	2.3028E-4	1.06532E-8	4	100.1
Nl-I	1.37533E-6	2.3796E-5	1.0482E-4	6.6921E-9	37	220.7
$R =$ II	2.10385E-6	2.11192E-4	4.6057E-4	4.2612E-8	4	100.9
NL-I	2.2417E-6	7.6871E-6	5.7134E-6	1.9983E-8	81	405.82
$R = 5$						
L-II	1.0509E-5	1.0561E-3	2.3027E-3	1.06385E-6	4	101.76
NL-I	3.2782E-7	2.8938E-4	2.1308E-4	3.63596E-7	116	632.6

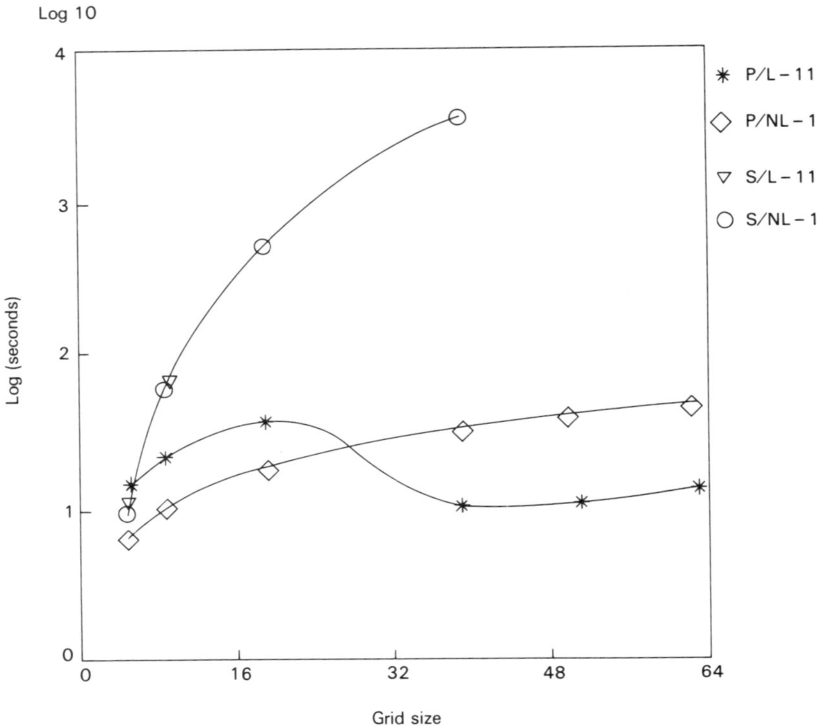

Graph 5.4 $R = 500$ against grid sizes up to 64×64, for parallel runs (P/L-II and P/NL-I) and sequential runs (S/L-II and S/NL-I).

the problem whereas the DAP achieved *the same solution in 34 s*; this is a speed-up of approximately 106. The version L-II could not be run at 19×19 because of insufficient main store on the DEC 1091. This demonstrates how easy it is to solve much larger problems on the DAP in this form.

We have now shown that the second formulation is in fact faster than the first, the Newton linearised version shows an improvement over the non-linear conjugate gradients and the DAP is considerably faster than the sequential machine. Let us now move on to examine the one remaining assumption that we made at the beginning of this section, that of preconditioning.

In section 5.6 we described a method for preconditioning a system of equations by diagonally scaling the matrix A such that our eigenvalues are more tighlty clustered. This approach was adopted in version L-II 1(section 5.4) when we employed our linear conjugate gradient solver; the results are given in Tables 5.9 and 5.10 (for 5×5 and 9×9 respectively). The linear iterations given are the

Table 5.7 $R = 500$ as n ranges from 5 to 63 for the ICL DAP.

	Error			Function value	Iterations	CPU time (s)
	U	Ux1	Ux2			
$N = 5$						
L-II	9.3132E-9	2.9868E-5	6.4599E-5	3.3829E-10	3	14.02
Nl-I	3.9339E-6	5.9451E-5	1.26476E-4	1.83641E-9	6	6.37
$N = 9$						
L-II	2.50762E-7	5.80493E-6	2.0283E-5	5.9363E-10	3	21.65
NL-I	6.62878E-7	5.94607E-5	1.2758E-4	1.77241E-9	10	10.57
$N = 19$						
L-II	3.3947E-7	8.5199E-6	2.1766E-5	1.5452E-9	3	37.85
NL-I	1.2144E-6	6.0716E-6	1.2899E-4	1.88079E-9	19	18.18
$N = 39$						
L-II	2.6177E-6	6.0993E-5	1.33705E-4	1.71386E-9	2	10.15
NL-I	7.262E-7	6.1537E-5	1.2953E-4	2.16312E-9	35	33.99
$N = 51$						
L-II	2.13668E-6	6.15899E-5	1.3081E-4	4.40314E-9	2	11.18
NL-I	6.3423E-7	6.2021E-5	1.2973E-4	2.3846E-9	42	40.94
$N = 65$						
L-II	2.47173E-7	6.28994E-5	1.25383E-4	1.12513E-8	2	13.21
NL-I	7.6091E-7	6.19706E-5	1.2972E-4	2.3978E-9	52	50.76

Table 5.8 Same as for Table 5.7 but for the sequential machine.

	Error			Function value	Iterations	CPU time (s)
	U	UX1	UX2			
$N = 5$						
L-I	1.4551E-8	3.0598E-5	6.4509E-5	3.3178E-10	3	11.56
NL-I	3.9335E-6	5.9451E-5	1.2647E-4	1.8363E-9	6	9.15
$N = 9$						
L-II	1.6491E-7	1.0133E-5	2.2764E-5	1.0765E-10	3	69.39
NL-I	6.6179E-7	5.946E-5	1.2758E-4	1.7723E-9	10	66.30
$N = 19$						
NL-I	1.2119E-6	6.0716E-5	1.2898E-4	1.88068E-9	19	546.0
$N = 39$						
NL-I	7.2814E-7	6.1573E-5	1.2952E-4	2.1629E-9	35	3612

Table 5.9 $R = 50$, a grid size of 5×5 ($h = 0.125$) for the ICL DAP with and without linear scaling.

		Linear solver	
		Without scaling	With scaling
Iterations	1	30	28
	2	91	80
	3	140	116
CPU time (s)		20.74	19.65
Error	U	5.6996E-7	6.2957E-7
	UX1	3.0361E-4	3.0358E-4
	UX2	6.4078E-4	6.4111E-4
Function value		3.4022E-8	3.3807E-8

[a]The iterations given are the numbers of cumulative linear iterations.

Table 5.10 $R = 50$, a grid size of 9×9 ($h = 0.625$) for the ICL DAP with and without linear scaling.

		Linear solver	
		Without scaling	With scaling
Iterations	1	50	40
	2	177	149
	3	270	220
CPU time (s)		32.0	29.33
Error	U	1.9334E-6	1.8962E-6
	UX1	5.8956E-5	5.9001E-6
	UX2	2.0528E-4	2.0684E-4
Function value		5.8734E-8	5.9221E-8

[a]The iterations given are the number of cumulative linear iterations.

Table 5.11 Two-dimensional heat conduction problem, with and without scaling.

	Without scaling	With scaling
$K_x = 1, K_y = 1$, 64×64		
Iterations	339	244
CPU time (s)	5.17	3.75
$K_x = 100, K_y = 1$, 41×41		
Iterations	1397	1101
CPU time (s)	20.1	15.06
$K_x = 100, K_y = 1$, 64×64		
Iterations	1768	1575
CPU time (s)	24.1	21.48

cumulative total after each call to the linear solver has been successfully completed and we can see a definite advantage in doing this form of preconditioning.

It was also decided to apply this preconditioning to the two-dimensional heat conduction problem described in Chapter 4, the results are given in Table 5.11. These also show a considerable advantage in using this form of scaling.

5.9 CONCLUSIONS

In this chapter we have successfully illustrated the fact that non-linear p.d.e.s can be mapped onto the DAP using a least-squares approach with several different formulations. These can then be subsequently solved very effectively on the DAP, when compared with a typical sequential machine.

In the next chapter we shall show how we can deal with problems which at first sight do not appear to map onto the DAP's grid of processors.

CHAPTER 6

Some Comments on More Complex Problems

6.1 INTRODUCTION

In the previous chapters of this book we have described the work done in implementing the solution process of linear and non-linear p.d.e.s on the DAP. Two questions that can immediately be posed are as follows. What should be done if the problem requires a grid size which is larger than the DAP's 64 × 64? What should be done if a problem requires a non-square region? Let us now look at each of these in turn and illustrate solution methods by reference to the two-dimensional heat conduction equation described earlier in Chapter 4.

6.2 PROBLEMS LARGER THAN THE DAP

In this section the method will be extended to problems requiring a grid size of up to $N \times N$, where $N = 128$, as shown in Fig. 6.1.

In such problems the number of processors in the DAP can be one-quarter of the number of elements in the problem to be solved. The approach to the solution adopted is called sheet mapping and, as shown above, the problem is divided into a number of 64 × 64 sheets. There is an alternative approach called crinkled mapping, in which a 2 × 2 neighbourhood of nodes or elements would be mapped into each PE. However, the former appeared to be more easily implemented within the existing code.

Indeed, if the problem is considered to be composed of four distinct segments, then with some extra manipulation on the segment

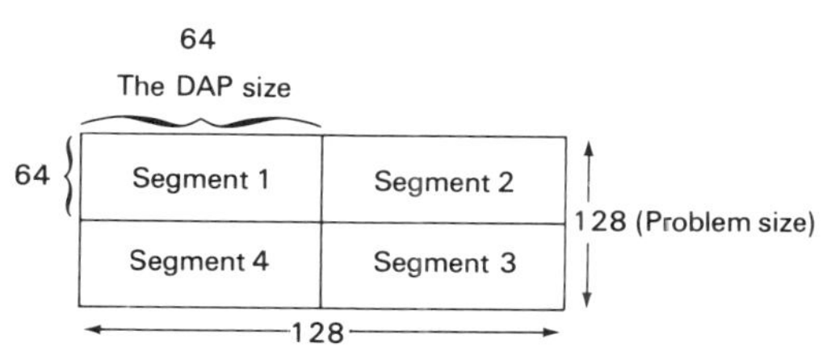

Fig. 6.1

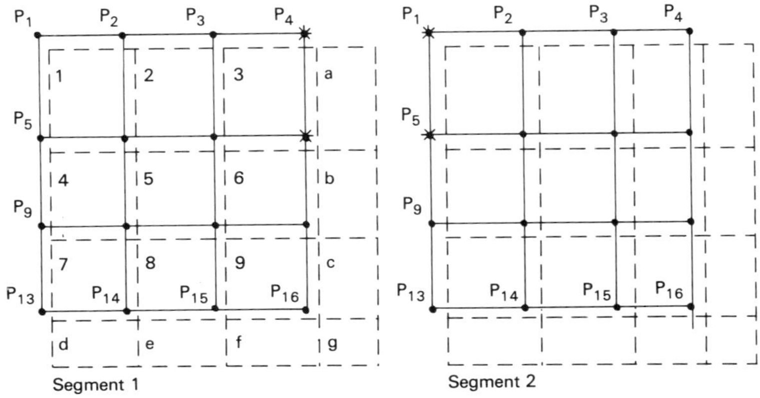

Fig. 6.2

boundaries (as opposed to the problem boundaries) the problem can be effectively solved with only slight modifications to the existing code.

There are two ways in which these segments can be connected.

For the first connection (form I) consider Fig. 6.2; for ease of illustration, imagine an $n \times n$ DAP, where $n = 4$, and consider just segments 1 and 2.

Each hard-lined grid represents the $n \times n$ set of nodes while the dashed grid represents the $(n - 1) \times (n - 1)$ set of elements. Note that the last row and column of elements are unused. In order to connect segments 1 and 2, use could be made of element a, it could be associated with the four nodes demonstrated by an asterisk (*), and similarly for the remainder of the segment boundary. However, when setting up the element information for element a (and other segment boundary elements), information is required from at least two nodes (three nodes for element g) which are not in the current matrix plane. For this reason it was decided to look at an alternative approach; this will be termed form II and is described below. Consider Fig. 6.3.

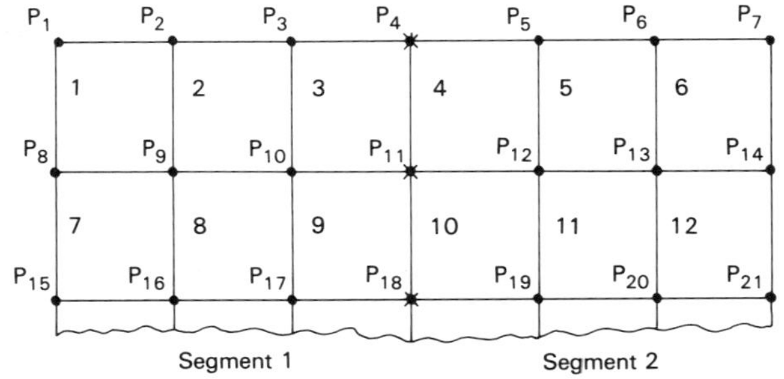

Fig. 6.3

In this form, imagine the segments being pushed together until they touch; the nodes indicated by an asterisk are actually stored in both segments. This approach to the connection of the segments reduces the maximum grid size available to $(N-1) \times (N-1)$ with a set of $(N-2) \times (N-2)$ elements, but this has the obvious advantage of allowing us to use existing code for setting up all the element information without having the problem of obtaining two or more values from another segment, as in the previous case. This form also has its own disadvantages; that is, because the nodes on adjoining segment boundaries are stored twice (node P_4, P_{11}, P_{18}, etc.), care must be taken when, in the conjugate gradient algorithm, products of the form $\mathbf{f}^T \cdot \mathbf{f}$ and $\mathbf{p}^T \cdot A\mathbf{p}$ are required for example. The two following points should also be noted.

(1) In a vector product $\mathbf{f}^T \cdot \mathbf{f}$ the values f_4, f_{11}, f_{18}, . . . must not be contributed twice.

(2) In the product $\mathbf{p}^T \cdot A\mathbf{p}$, the product $\mathbf{r} = A\mathbf{p}$ is formed first and then the values of $\mathbf{r}$ are placed at the correct global positions (achieved exactly as described in Chapter 4). However, because the segments are only conceptually linked together and not physically linked, then the contribution for $\mathbf{r}$ at node P_{11} (the contribution coming from elements 3, 4, 9 and 10) say, will be in two separate segments, as shown in Fig. 6.4. These values in the two separate segments must then be added together to form a correct value for r_{11} *but* bearing in mind point (1) which will apply to forming the final product $\mathbf{p}^T \cdot \mathbf{r}$. This is illustrated in Fig. 6.4.

These difficulties may indeed seem to be more complicated than those of form I but the actual changes to the existing code are only slight and it was this form which was chosen for the implementation. It must be stressed that all the mathematical formulations and

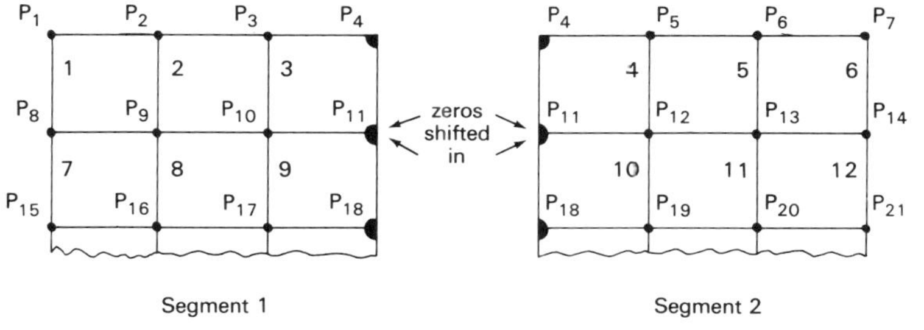

Fig. 6.4

algorithms of Chapter 4 remain exactly the same. Results for problems up to 127 × 127 in size will be given.

6.2.1 Results

Since the purpose of this section is to illustrate the relative ease with which problems larger than the size of the DAP can be implemented, we confined our testing to the simplest case with the conductivities K_x and K_y set equal to 1. The strength of the source and sink points and their relative locations are given in Table 6.1 at the end of this chapter. All the tests were terminated when $\mathbf{f}^T \cdot \mathbf{f} < 1e - 12$, and a saftey check was imposed on the number of iterations. The results are given in Table 6.2 but for illustrative purposes these can be more easily seen in Graph 6.1 where the logarithm of time is plotted against grid size. The jump in the graph which occurs at 65 × 65, that is the point at which the DAP's grid size is exceeded, is caused both by an organisational overhead (a factor of 4 from the number of DAP sheets) and by an increase in the number of iterations. This organisational overhead will also be present at all multiples of the DAP's grid size.

An alternative way of looking at this is to plot the relative efficiency against grid size, where relative efficiency is obtained by

$$\frac{\text{number of processors in use}}{\text{total number of processors}} \times 100$$

and this is illustrated by the 'sawtooth' effect seen in Graph 6.2. This graph can be continued and we see that, each time that the problem exceeds a multiple of the DAP, the efficiency drops but the percentage to which it drops increases each time.

Table 6.1 Strength of sources and sinks and their locations.

N \ Q	1.0	0.5	0.6	−1.83	−0.27
11	(2, 2, 1)	(2, 10, (1)	(8, 2, 1)	(6, 6, 1)	(10, 10, 1)
21	(2, 2, 1)	(2, 20, 1)	(14, 3, 1)	(10, 11, 1)	(20, 20, 1)
31	(3, 3, 1)	(3, 27, 1)	(23, 4, 1)	(14, 15, 1)	(27, 27, 1)
41	(6, 6, 1)	(6, 36, 1)	(28, 6, 1)	(20, 20, 1)	(36, 36, 1)
64, 65	(9, 9, 1)	(9, 60, 1)	(54, 9, 1)	(34, 34, 1)	(60, 60, 1)
70	(10, 10, 1)	(10, 3, 2)	(60, 10, 1)	(37, 37, 1)	(3, 3, 3)
80	(15, 15, 1)	(15, 15, 2)	(62, 15, 1)	(45, 45, 1)	(15, 15, 3)
100	(20, 20, 1)	(20, 26, 2)	(16, 20, 4)	(60, 60, 1)	(26, 26, 3)
127	(22, 22, 1)	(22, 56, 2)	(44, 22, 4)	(4, 4, 3)	(56, 56, 3)

Termination is on $\sqrt{(\mathbf{f}^T \cdot \mathbf{f})} < 1e - 6$, as in Chapter 4.

Table 6.2 Solution times.

$N \times N$	Iterations	CPU time (s)
11	46	1.06
21	85	1.61
31	125	2.18
41	205	3.32
64	339	5.17
65	513	30.14
70	1013	58.01
80	1345	76.64
100	1875	106.40
127	2417	136.76

It should be stressed that despite the organisational overhead there is still a very considerable time advantage over the sequential version which had to be stopped at 41 × 41 because of restrictions on overall storage.

The second question that posed was as follows. How can problems which are of a non-square domain be solved? In the section 6.3, this question will be discussed.

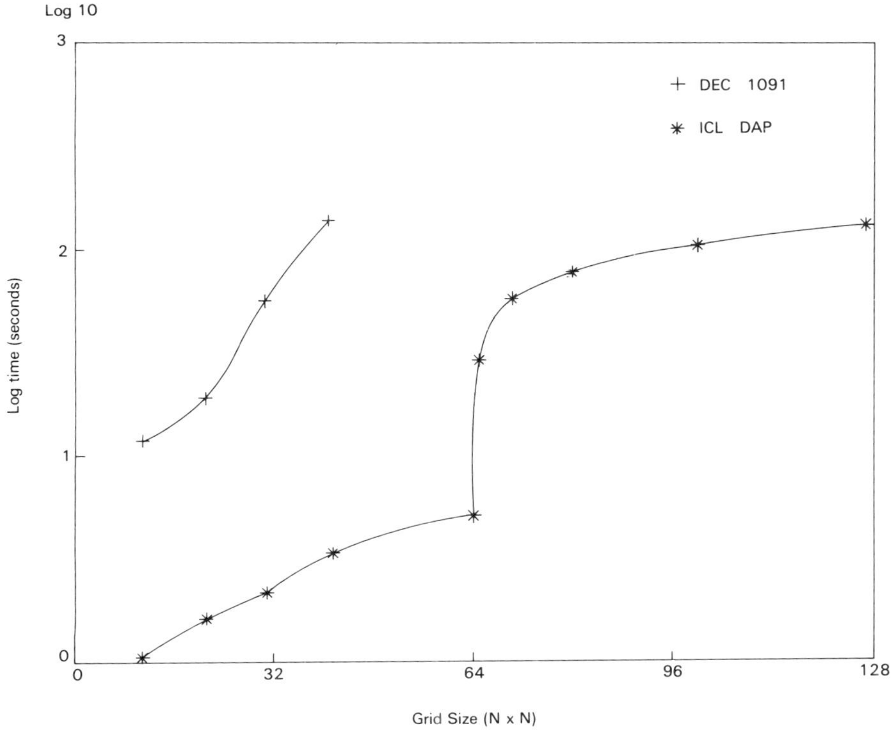

Graph 6.1

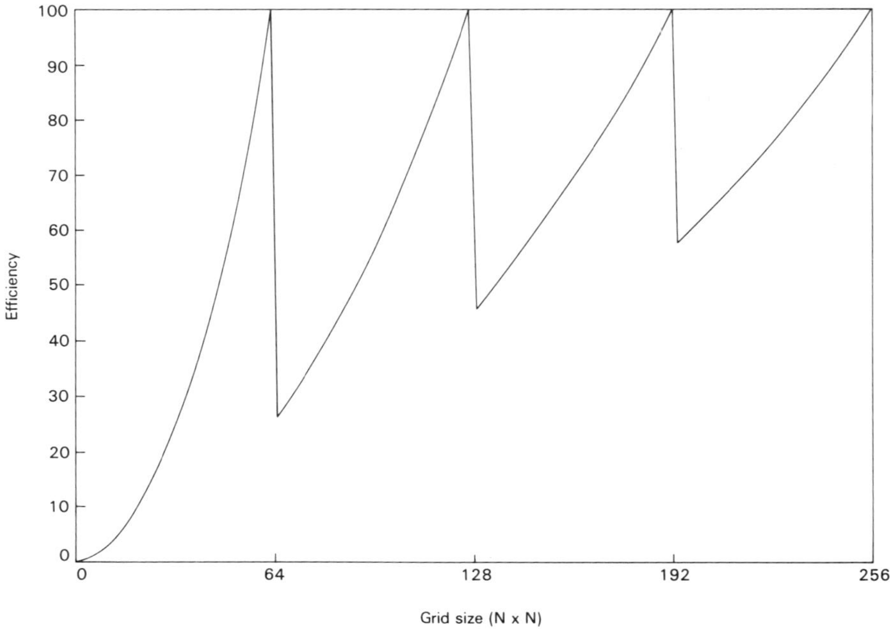

Graph 6.2

6.3 NON-SQUARE PROBLEMS

The DAP's ability to deactivate particular processors makes the solution of the non-square problems extremely effective. The region examined was the L shape illustrated below in Fig. 6.5.

Again all the mathematical formulations and algorithms remain unchanged from those in Chapter 4 and there was no refinement of the mesh at point $(\frac{3}{4}, \frac{1}{4})$. The important point that must be stressed is that the algorithm and code have remained exactly as described in Chapter 4, except for the creation of a logical mask with TRUE

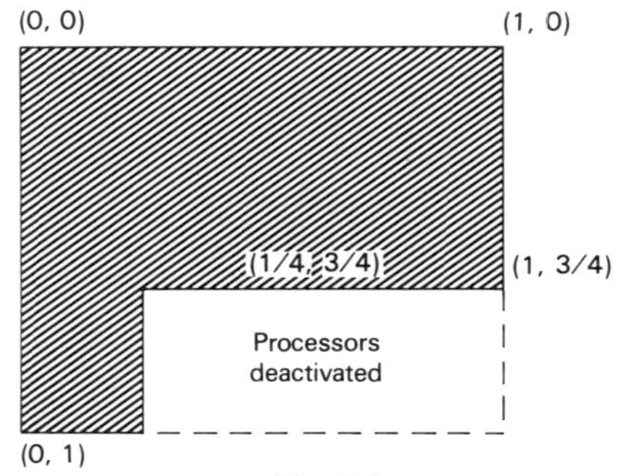

Fig. 6.5

values inside the L shape and FALSE values outside. This effectively deactivates certain processors. The results obtained will now be given.

6.3.1 Results

The conductivities K_x and K_y were both set to 1 and the source and sink points used are given in Table 6.3. For comparison purposes a sequential version was tested using a similar strategy to the DAP, that is set up a square region and then process only the work that

Table 6.3

N \ Q	1.0	0.5	0.6	−1.85	−0.27
12	(2, 2)	(2, 10)	(8, 2)	(6, 6)	(7, 9)
24	(4, 4)	(4, 20)	(16, 4)	(12, 12)	(14, 18)
36, 41	(6, 6)	(6, 30)	(24, 6)	(18, 18)	(21, 27)
48	(8, 8)	(8, 40)	(32, 8)	(24, 24)	(28, 36)
64	(10, 10)	(10, 50)	(40, 10)	(30, 30)	(35, 45)

Table 6.4 Non-square region.

N	Iterations		Time (s)	
	DEC	DAP	DEC	DAP
12	47	49	12.56	1.07
24	87	94	40.44	1.69
36	129	139	126.3	2.31
41	149	156	138.5	2.54
48	—	184	—	2.92
64	—	327	—	4.87

Table 6.5 Square region.

N	Iterations		Time (s)	
	DEC	DAP	DEC	DAP
11	46	46	11.7	1.06
21	85	85	18.8	1.61
31	125	125	58.1	2.18
41	167	205	137.1	3.32
64	—	339	—	5.17

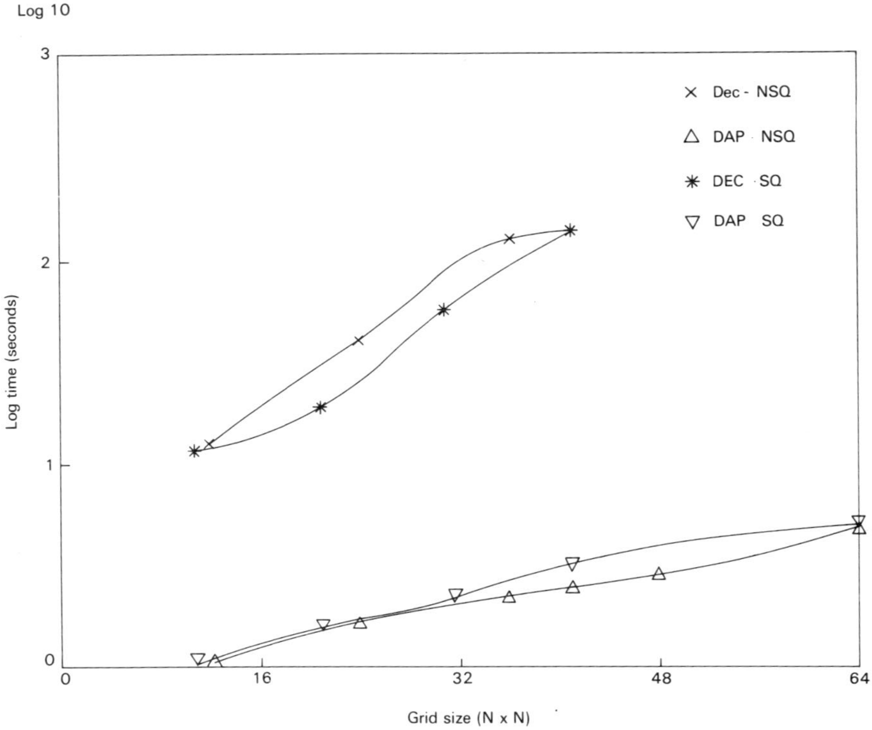

Graph 6.3

occurs in the region of interest. In effect the only difference between the parallel and sequential codes are that, where the DAP has a logical mask with FALSE values to switch off processors outside the L shape, the sequential code tests each element for its position inside the square region but outside the L shape and performs a conditional jump. The results in Tables 6.4 and 6.5 show that there is very little difference between the two times (non-square and square). In Graph 6.3 where the logarithm of time is plotted against grid size, these data are illustrated more effectively, where SQ indicates the square region and NSQ the non-square region.

6.3.2 Conclusions

This chapter has described how some of the main problems which are normally raised when the possibility of using the DAP is discussed can be effectively overcome.

It has been shown that the current size of the DAP does not limit the size of the problem; larger problems can be mapped onto the array of processors. Secondly, the shape of the DAP does not limit the shape of the problem; non-rectangular problems can also be mapped onto the array of processors.

In the next chapter it will be shown that the Navier–Stokes class of problems can also be solved on the DAP.

CHAPTER 7

The Navier–Stokes Equations

7.1 INTRODUCTION

In Chapter 5 of this book, two different least-squares formulations of the non-linear Morgan problem were described. The non-linear conjugate gradient and truncated Newton algorithms which were used to complete the solution to the problem were then described.

In this chapter, this approach will be extended to a particular Navier–Stokes equation in two dimensions. The solution will be achieved by a least-squares non-linear conjugate gradient approach.

7.2 THE PROBLEM

The two-dimensional Navier–Stokes equation is given by

$$u \frac{\partial u}{\partial x_1} + v \frac{\partial u}{\partial x_2} = -\frac{\partial p}{\partial x_1} + \frac{1}{R} \nabla^2 u$$

$$u \frac{\partial v}{\partial x_1} + v \frac{\partial v}{\partial x_2} = -\frac{\partial p}{\partial x_2} + \frac{1}{R} \nabla^2 v$$

$$\frac{\partial u}{\partial x_1} + \frac{\partial v}{\partial x_2} = 0$$

subject to some suitable boundary conditions and where u is the component of velocity in x, v is the component of velocity in x_2, p is the pressure and R is the Reynolds number.

7.3 THE LEAST-SQUARES FORMULATION

By the least-squares finite element method the solution to this problem can be written as

$$\min I = \int \mathbf{e}^{\mathrm{T}} \cdot W\mathbf{e} \, \mathrm{d}V \tag{7.4}$$

where $\mathbf{e} = (e_1, e_2, \ldots, e_n)$ and which is subject to some boundary conditions. If we now introduce the set of new variables

$$A = u, \qquad B = \frac{\partial u}{\partial x_1}, \qquad C = \frac{\partial u}{\partial x_2}$$

$$D = v, \qquad E = \frac{\partial v}{\partial x_1}, \qquad F = \frac{\partial v}{\partial x_2}$$

$$P = p, \qquad G = \frac{\partial p}{\partial x_1}, \qquad H = \frac{\partial p}{\partial x_2}$$

then the Navier–Stokes equations defined in section 7.2 can be reduced to the following set of first-order equations:

$$e_1 = AB + CD - \frac{1}{R}\left(\frac{\partial B}{\partial x_1} + \frac{\partial C}{\partial x_2}\right) + \frac{\partial P}{\partial x_1} = 0$$

$$e_2 = AE + DF - \frac{1}{R}\left(\frac{\partial E}{\partial x_1} + \frac{\partial F}{\partial x_2}\right) + \frac{\partial P}{\partial x_2} = 0$$

$$e_3 = B + F = 0$$

$$e_4 = \frac{\partial A}{\partial x_1} - B = 0$$

$$e_5 = \frac{\partial A}{\partial x_2} - C = 0$$

$$e_6 = \frac{\partial D}{\partial x_1} - E = 0$$

$$e_7 = \frac{\partial D}{\partial x_2} - F = 0$$

By introducing the set of shape functions which have been previously defind in Chapter 5 the following approximations are achieved:

$$A = \sum a_i\phi_i, \qquad B = \sum b_i\phi_i, \qquad C = \sum c_i\phi_i,$$

$$D = \sum d_i\phi_i, \qquad E = \sum e_i\phi_i, \qquad F = \sum f_i\phi_i$$

$$P = \sum p_i\phi_i, \qquad G = \sum g_i\phi_i, \qquad H = \sum h_i\phi_i$$

These can now be substituted into the set of equations (7.6) to obtain the new set

$$e^1 = \sum a_j\phi_i \sum b_j\phi_j + \sum c_i\phi_i \sum d_j\phi_j$$

$$- \frac{1}{R}\left[\frac{\partial}{\partial x_1}\left(\sum b_i\phi_i\right) + \frac{\partial}{\partial x_2}\left(\sum c_i\phi_i\right)\right] + \frac{\partial}{\partial x_1}\left(\sum p_i\phi_i\right)$$

$$e_2 = \sum a_i\phi_i \sum e_j\phi_j + \sum d\ \phi_i \sum f\ \phi_j$$

$$- \frac{1}{R}\left[\frac{\partial}{\partial x_1}\left(\sum e_i\phi_i\right) + \frac{\partial}{\partial x_2}\left(\sum f_i\phi_i\right)\right] + \frac{\partial}{\partial x_2}\left(\sum p_i\phi_i\right)$$

$$e_3 = \sum b_i\phi_i + \sum f_i\phi_i$$

$$e_4 = \sum a_i \frac{\partial \phi_i}{\partial x_1} - \sum b_i\phi_i$$

$$e_5 = \sum a_i \frac{\partial \phi_i}{\partial x_2} - \sum c_i\phi_i$$

$$e_6 = \sum d_i \frac{\partial \phi_i}{\partial x_1} - \sum e_i\phi_i$$

$$e_7 = \sum d_i \frac{\partial \phi_i}{\partial x_2} - \sum f_i\phi_i$$

As mentioned in Section 7.1, the solution is completed using a non-linear conjugate gradient algorithm. In section 7.4 we shall describe why this is the only algorithm that can be used.

7.4 SOLUTION ALGORITHM

In Chapter 5 a version of the truncated Newton algorithm was described. However, if this algorithm were used for the Navier–Stokes problem, there would be difficulties with storage of the element matrices, as follows.

The element matrices are 28 × 28 in size (four nodes per element and seven unknowns per node), thus requiring 784 real (32-bit) values per element. This on its own is too large for the storage on the DAP which currently is

$$16\text{K}/32 \text{ bits per real} = 512$$

An alternative would have been to make use of the symmetry of the element matrices by storing just the upper triangle. This method would require

$$\sum_{i=1}^{28} i = 406 + \text{other working store}$$

Unfortunately the 'other working store' required (element information to form gradient **g**, line search, solution algorithm, etc.) makes this approach also infeasible.

For these reasons it was decided to confine the examination of the Navier–Stokes equation on the DAP to the non-linear conjugate gradient algorithm developed earlier in section 5.3. For this method the total storage requirement is approximately of the order of 6K bits per processor.

In addition to this it was decided that because of the complexity of the Navier–Stokes class of problems a form of mesh refinement would be utilised; this will now be described.

7.5 MESH REFINEMENT

For this work the approach that was taken was to commence the solution process with a small grid having relatively few unknowns. Starting from an initial solution of zero, the algorithm would be allowed to converge to some suitable criterion; the mesh would then be refined with the intial solution for the new mesh coming from the previous final solution plus the interpolated points.

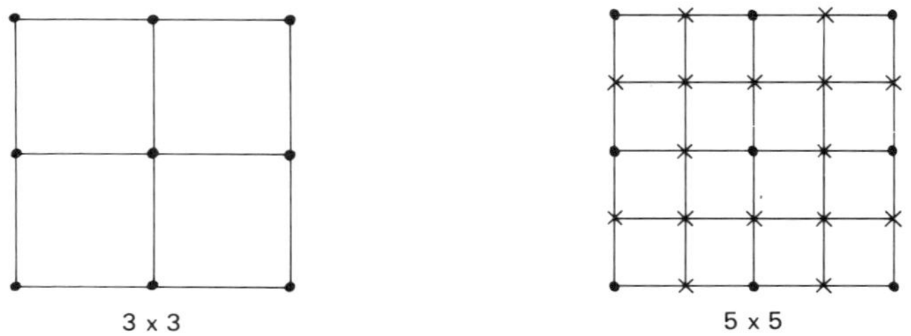

Fig. 7.1

Consider Fig. 7.1. Here a 3 × 3 mesh is refined into a 5 × 5 mesh; the points denoted by full circles are the original solution points, whilst those denoted by crosses are the new interpolated points and are obtained as follows.

Given an element, it is required to interpolate the five new points indicated in Fig. 7.2 using the local coordinate points (γ, η) with the shape functions. Therefore any new point u_I can be obtained from the expression

$$u_I = \sum_{i=1}^{4} \phi_i(\gamma, \eta)u_i$$

where ϕ_i is defined by

$$\phi_1 = \frac{(1 + \gamma)(1 + \eta)}{4}$$

$$\phi_2 = \frac{(1 - \gamma)(1 + \eta)}{4}$$

$$\phi_3 = \frac{(1 - \gamma)(1 - \eta)}{4}$$

$$\phi_4 = \frac{(1 + \gamma)(1 - \eta)}{4}$$

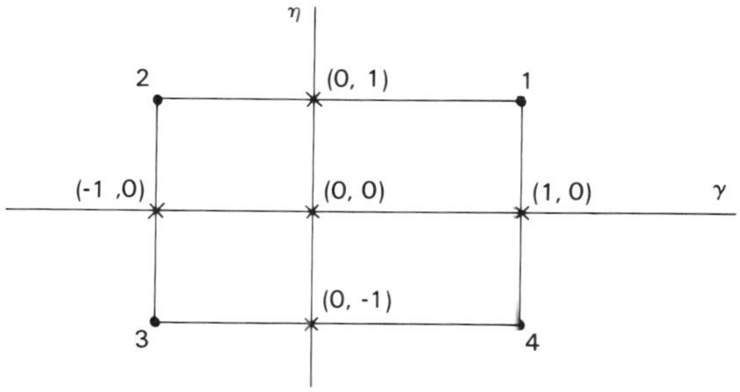

Fig. 7.2

It is very easily seen that this process of interpolation can be achieved in parallel, and the interpolation has no effect on the function value I; it is simply used as a means of improving an initial solution. For details of this refer to Section A 4.1.

In section 7.6 the problem used and the results obtained will be given.

7.6 TEST PROBLEM: A SQUARE CAVITY

This test was to study the flow inside a square cavity which is shown in Fig. 7.3.

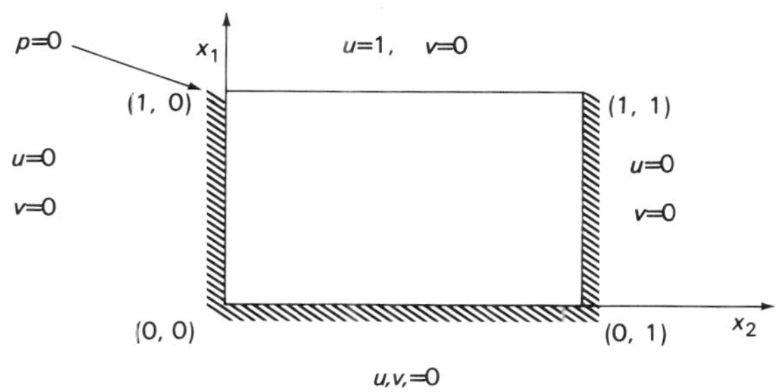

Fig. 7.3

7.7 RESULTS

The initial results obtained for this work are given in Table 7.1 for a Reynolds number of 1.0 with the initial solution being taken to be zero and with no interpolation from a previous mesh. These results showed that, as the mesh is successively refined, the function value I in fact increases, where it is normally expected to decrease.

An explanation of these results can be given by examining Fig. 7.3. At the points (1, 0) and (1, 1) there are two discontinuities

Table 7.1

Mesh		Sequential	Parallel
5 × 5	Function value	0.386888	0.3868921
	Function calls	371	357
	Iterations	186	178
	CPU time	3 min 49.93 s	5 min 50.4 s
9 × 9	Function value	0.687364	0.687375
	Function calls	906	856
	Iterations	450	424
	CPU time	32 min 22.66 s	13 min 59.8 s
21 × 21	Function value		1.09953
	Function calls		2803
	Iterations		1315
	CPU time		44 min 42.56 s

The Reynolds number equals 1.0. Termination on $\mathbf{g}^T \cdot \mathbf{g} < 1e{-}6$. 5 × 5 mesh has 142 unknowns, 9 × 9 mesh has 502 unknowns and 21 × 21 mesh has 2926 unknowns after allowing for fixed boundary points. The initial function value for a 3 × 3 mesh is 2.0. The results are for sequential times on a DEC 1091.

Table 7.2

	3 × 3	5 × 5	9 × 9	17 × 17
Function value	0.2037	0.080917	0.0353309	0.017301
CPU time	2 min 56 s	5 min 39 s	14 min 11 s	13 min 51 s
Total CPU time	36 min 37 s			
Iterations	82	164	417	389

The Reynolds number equals 1.0. Termination on $\mathbf{g}^T \cdot \mathbf{g} < 1e{-}6$. 5 × 5 mesh has 142 unknowns, 9 × 9 mesh has 502 unknowns and 21 × 21 mesh has 2926 unknowns after allowing for fixed boundary points. The initial function value for a 3 × 3 mesh is 2.0. The results are for sequential times on a DEC 1091.

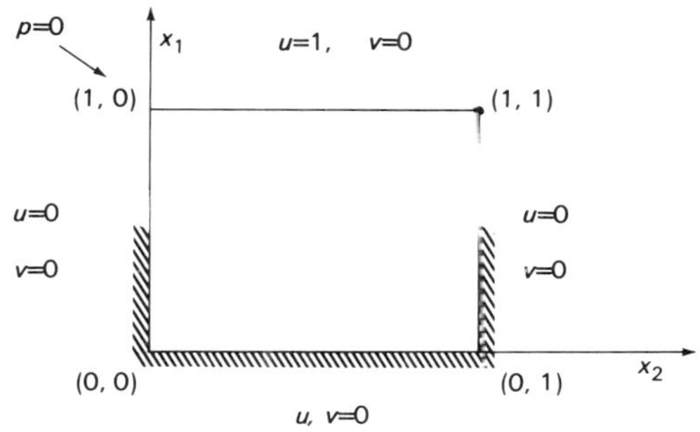

Fig. 7.4

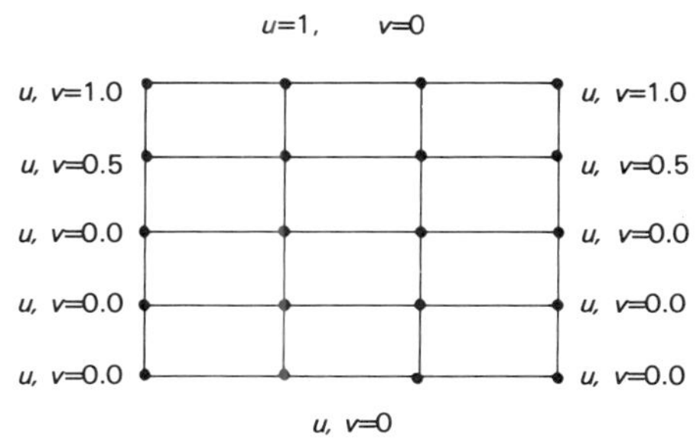

Fig. 7.5

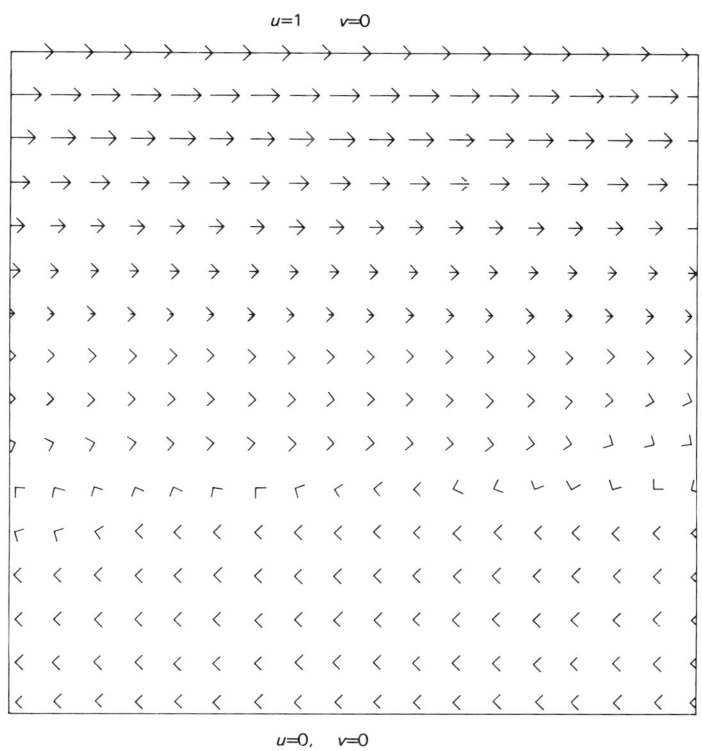

Fig. 7.6 Flow diagram corresponding to the problem described in Fig. 7.4. Produced at The Hatfield Polytechnic using a standard graphical package.

of flow. These singularities prevent the function value I from being reduced; further details are given in Section A4.2.

It seems natural to remove these two singularities. This is achieved by redefining the boundary conditions about those two points, to give Fig. 7.4. The profile of flow in this problem has in effect been altered and a linear boundary condition of the form $u = \alpha + \beta y$ introduced.

The effect of these new boundary conditions for a 5×5 mesh will give the result in Fig. 7.5. The results for the new problem described in Fig. 7.4 are given in Table 7.2 and here the interpolation was introduced. The solution was started at a 3×3 mesh and successively refined up to a 17×17. Here it can be seen that the function value I is successively reduced, once the singularities have been removed. Fig. 7.6 illustrates the flow over the region, which is heavily dominated in the upper half. The reason for this is that the new boundary conditions were imposed at the mesh of 5×5 and therefore remain at the same relative positions as the mesh is refined. Had these conditions been imposed at an initial size of 9×9, then the central line would effectively move up to approximately the three-quarter position.

CHAPTER 8

Conclusions and Future Research

8.1 CONCLUSIONS

In the previous chapters (and the appendixes) of this book the research which was undertaken has been described in some detail; the conclusions which have been previously drawn will now be summarised.

All classes of parallel computers will offer some improvement in terms of computational time over a typical sequential machine, provided of course that a given problem is suitable for the particular type of architecture concerned. This research has been confined to a detailed study of just how advantageous it is to use the DAP, for the reasons given in Chapter 1.

In Chapter 4 the solution of the self-adjoint two-dimensional heat conduction equation on the DAP was described. The approach adopted followed the Galerkin finite element method with the assembly of the global stiffness matrix being avoided. Results showed that a speed-up factor of over 40 could be achieved on the DAP for a problem with 1681 equations; this would naturally have been larger had it been possible to solve a problem with 4096 equations on the sequential computer used for a comparison.

In Chapter 5 the solution of a non-linear p.d.e (the Morgan problem) was considered using a least-squares finite element method. Two different mathematical formulations were used and the solution completed using both a non-linear conjugate gradient and a truncated Newton method. The most striking result for this problem was that, when solving on a 39×39 mesh with the non-linear conjugate gradient code, the speed-up was of the order 106 at a point were we are effectively using only three-eighths of the DAP. When using the Newton method it is required to solve a series of linear problems; for this the linear conjugate gradient code developed in Chapter 4 was used. In conjunction with this method a preconditioning was experimented with; the approach chosen was a diagonal scaling of the system which achieved some favourable results.

In Chapter 6 it was effectively shown how problems both larger than the DAP and with non-square boundaries can easily be solved with minimal changes to the standard 64×64 code.

Chapter 7 of this book was confined to looking at a solution of a Navier–Stokes problem, namely flow over a square cavity in two dimensions. This also gave some interesting results concerning two singularities which exist in the definition of the problem. These singularities were then removed by redefining the boundaries and the new problem was solved.

The work described in this book has been concerned with the ICL DAP. However, the machine used was constructed at the beginning of a new era of processors and therefore naturally as a prototype; it is expensive and available to only a few research workers. A new generation of DAPs such as Mil-DAPs are becoming available; these are compact stand-alone machines with low power requirements and already super-Mil-DAPs are being planned. For Further reading on these machines and applications those interested are referred to [1] (and in particular the paper by Simpson and Merrifield [2]).

In section 8.2, future research which would be a natural extension to this work will be described.

8.2 FUTURE RESEARCH

The future research which can be currently visualised in this field falls into three categories.

The first is a form of mesh refinement similar to that described in Chapter 7 for solving the Navier–Stokes equations. In this chapter an approach was described in which the process is started by solving a comparatively small mesh with relatively few unknowns and then by employing interpolation, successively refining the mesh using the final solution from the previous mesh as the initial solution for the refined mesh. This may be particularly useful both for solving the Navier–Stokes equations when there is a large Reynolds number and for a non-square problem similar to that described in section 6.3. Particular care will be necessary, however, in handling the boundary conditions if the full benefit of this approach is to be attained.

The second category for future research could be in seeking a suitable form of preconditioner which would map readily onto both the non-linear conjugate gradient algorithm and the DAP.

The final aspect of the future research could be in developing a method which would be suitable for solving three-dimensional p.d.e.s by the finite element approach described in the previous chapters of this book. This would of course be considerably more difficult in respect of the fact that the DAP has a two-dimensional interconnectivity of processors compared with the problem's three-dimensional connectivity, as illustrated by Wait and Martindale [3].

Appendix 1

A1.1 INTRODUCTION

In Chapter 1 the initial work on the problems of locating a global minimum of an unconstrained multi-extremal function was mentioned; the implementation on the ICL DAP will now be described.

A1.2 THE PROBLEM

The problem of global optimisation is as follows:

$$\min F(x) \qquad x \in S \subset R^n$$

where

$$S = \{x : a_i \leqslant x_i \leqslant b_i\}$$

Assuming that the function $F(x)$ is non-convex and has more than one local minimum, then the problem is to isolate the point x with the least function value (which is by definition the global minimum).

An international study comparing the relative efficiency of a number of programs for the solution of the global optimisation problem has been reported by Dixon and Szego [1]. That study indicated that most of the efficient codes are based on probabilistic principles and that the heuristic CRS algorithm proposed by Price [2] was one of the most successful. He has recently proposed a simplified version [3] and this was chosen for implementation on the parallel system.

The probabilistic method of solution relies on the following assumption. If a finite number of points are chosen at random and are uniformly distributed in the region S, then, if A is a subset of S with a measure m such that

$$\frac{m(A)}{m(S)} \geqslant \alpha \geqslant 0$$

and $p(A, N)$ is probability that at least one point of a sequence of N random points lies in A,

$$\lim_{N \to \infty} \mathrm{p}(A, N) = 1$$

The heuristic method selects N points at random and then aims at improving the best points located in the random search.

A1.3 PRICE'S ALGORITHM FOR THE ICL DAP

The sequential algorithm of Price which would be suitable for running on an ICL DAP for small values of n has been described by Dixon and Patel [4]. This has now been implemented and the main features of this algorithm are contained in the flow chart in Fig. A1.1.

Briefly what happens is this; $3n \times 4096$ (64×64) points are generated over the domain S and their function values determined. ($3n$ points are allocated to each processor, n being the dimension of the problem.) The largest-valued n points per processor are then rejected and the overall 4096 remaining largest points are chosen, one being placed in each processor.

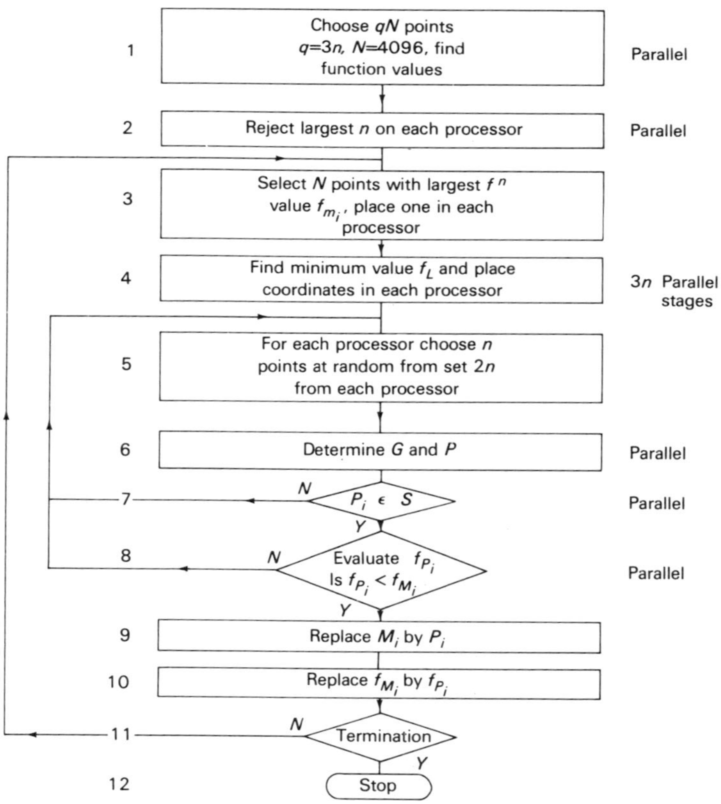

Fig. A1.1

In order to generate new trial points P_i, $n \times 4096$ points are chosen at random from the remaining set of $2n \times 4096$ (n points coming from each processor). These points together with the minimum point f_L are used to determine the centroid followed by the new trial point matrix P.

Suppose n points $R_2, R_3, \ldots, R_{n+1}$ have been chosen at random and $R, = L$ then

$$\mathbf{G} = \left(\sum_{i=1}^{n} \mathbf{R}_i\right) \Big/ n$$

and

$$\mathbf{P} = 2\mathbf{G} - \mathbf{R}_{n+1}$$

If the new points generated are within the domain S then we evaluate $F(\mathbf{P})$; otherwise we must repeat by choosing more points at random, for those which are not within S. We also repeat from this stage if $F(\mathbf{F})$ is worse than the existing point.

At this stage (after one or possibly more iterations) we have a full set of 4096 points which are contained within the domain S and whose function values are less than the corresponding maximum function values. It is these improved values that are used in the replacement process and the test for termination is carried out.

The termination criterion examines the three smallest values of the function; L_1, L_2, L_3 such that $L_1 < L_2 < L_3$ and then, if $|L_1 - L_2| < \varepsilon$ and $|L_2 - L_3| < \varepsilon$, the algorithm stops or otherwise the cycle is repeated by selecting the 4096 new largest values, etc.

In section A1.4, some of the initial results obtained are described and an explanation as to why they were not as good as one might originally have expected is given.

A1.4 INITIAL RESULTS

The results for the functions used (listed in Section A1.7, are given in Table A1.1 (sequential versus old parallel) and are rather disappointing. From the flowchart in Fig. A1.1 it is seen that there are three sections in the algorithm that had needed to be coded sequentially; these were in fact isolated as being the main time consumers. They were as follows.

(1) Step 3: when choosing the overall 4096 largest function values it was necessary to code it sequentially, namely to find the largest value, to mask it out, then to find the next, etc.
(2) Step 5 it proved to be extremely difficult to find a method for choosing n points at random for each processor in parallel, since

Table A1.1

Function	Sequential		New parallel		Old parallel		Gain
	CPU time (s)	Function calls	CPU time (s)	Function calls	CPU time (s)	Function calls	
Six-hump camel back (two global minima)	0.36 0.81 1.17	288 798 1086	0.093	8	95.6	21	12.5
Branin (three global minima)	0.47 0.97 1.73 3.17	360 654 1024 2038	0.118	8	25.7 25.8	9 9	26.8
Goldstein and Price (one global minima)	0.45	481	0.13	8	37.78	12	3.5
Hartmans (one global minimum) $n = 5$	0.88	503	0.276	11	67.33	13	3.2
Shekel (one global minimum) $m = 5$ $m = 7$ $m = 10$	3.89 3.82 4.31	2372 2423 2567	0.453 0.55 0.693	14 14 14	Not run Not run Not run		8.6 6.9 6.2
Shubert two dimensional (18 global minima)	Average 1.58 per minimum Total 15.8 995 function calls		0.233	7			68

The gain is the ratio of the parallel value to the sequential value.

it was a requirement that the n points be chosen at random, avoiding the points previously rejected and keeping track of where the chosen points had come from (eventually the coordinates were recorded as row, column, plane).

(3) Steps 9 and 10: when replacing the points M_i by new points P_i and similarly f_{M_i} by f_{P_i}, they had to be replaced in the positions from which they initially came.

These three points in the program were modified and the resulting new version of the algorithm is described in the section A1.5.

A1.5 MODIFIED PRICE'S ALGORITHM

The new algorithm is shown in the flow chart in Fig. A1.2 and is described in some more detail as follows.

(1) After rejecting the largest n points on each processor, we 'compact down' the matrices holding M_i and f_{M_i}; we now no longer require special code to avoid rejected values.
(2) Instead of choosing the overall 4096 maximum values, 4096 are

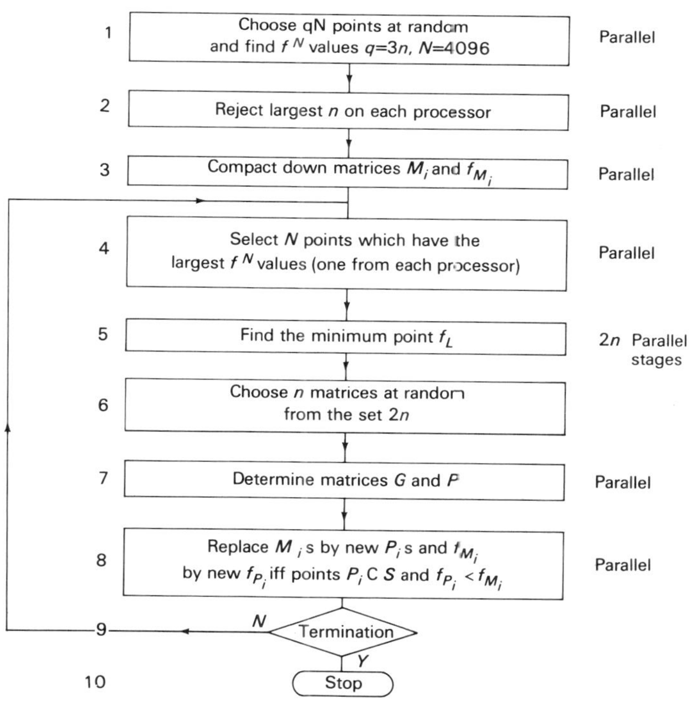

Fig. A1.2

now selected; one (the maximum from each processor) which can be done quite simply in parallel.

(3) Instead of choosing n points at random, one from each processor, n matrices are now chosen at random. This means that it is now no longer necessary to record the positions of the randomly selected points for later reference; they have all now come from one of n matrices.

(4) Since whole matrices are now chosen at random rather than as individual points, then the replacement of old by new is much simpler, that is a logical mask can be generated containing TRUE values only at positions where the new point is contained within the domain S *and* where the function value f_{P_i} is less than f_{M_i}. This mask can then be used in a series of assignments.

(5) When we compact down the two matrices there was space left over, n (real 32-bit) planes in F_{M_i}, and n^2 in M_i, this is now used for holding the centroids, the new trial points, the maximum values and the function values of new trial points.

A1.6 IMPROVED RESULTS AND CONCLUSIONS

On looking at the results from Table A1.1 (sequential versus new parallel), it is obvious that there is now a considerable improvement from the new algorithm.

A direct comparison of the times for the sequential and the new parallel yields the improvement factor which can be seen to range from 3.2 to 68. This considerable range can be explained by the fact that the lower improvement factors came from functions which had just one global minimum, whereas the larger factors came from the functions possessing multiple global minima. The best example is probably the Shubert function which has 18 global minima; the new algorithm picked up 11 of these in one run, whereas the sequential algorithm required 10 runs to pick up these same 11 minima.

It can also be seen that the number of parallel function evaluations needed has been drastically reduced compared with the sequential ones.

The CRS optimisation method described in [1], on which our method is based, is designed for thoroughness of search rather than for speed of convergence and where possible the global minima could be refined using faster methods.

By comparing the new and old parallel versions it is obvious that the parallelism in the algorithm must be very closely matched onto the available hardware, in order to take advantage of it.

A1.7 FUNCTIONS

(1) *Six-hump camel back function*

$$f(\mathbf{x}) = ax_1^2 + bx_1^4 + cx_1^6 - x_1x_2 + dx_2^2 + ex_2^4$$

where $a = 4, b = -2.1, c = \frac{1}{3}, d = -4$ and $e = 4$. The region of interest is $-3 \leqslant x_1 \leqslant 3, \; -2 \leqslant x_2 \leqslant 2$.

(2) *Branin*

$$f(\mathbf{x}) = a(x_2 - bx_1^2 + cx_1 - d)^2 + e(1 - f)\cos x_1 + e$$

where $a = 1, b = 5.1/4\pi^2, c = 5/\pi, d = 6, e = 10$ and $f = 1/8\pi$. The region of interest is $-5 \leqslant x_1 \leqslant 10, \; 0 \leqslant x_2 \leqslant 15$.

(3) *Coldstein and Price*

$$f(\mathbf{x}) = [1 + (x_1 + x_2 + 1)^2(19 - 14x_1 + 3x_1^2 - 14x_2 + 6x_1x_2 + 3x_2^2)] \times [30 + (2x_1 - 3x_2)^2(18 - 32x_1 + 12x_1^2 + 48x_2 - 36x_1x_2 + 27x_2^2)]$$

The region of interest is $-2 \leqslant x_{1,2} \leqslant 2$.

(4) *Hartmans*

$$f(\mathbf{x}) = -\sum_{i=1}^{m} c_i \exp\left[-\sum_{j=1}^{n} \alpha_{ij}(x_j - p_{ij})\right]$$

$\mathbf{x} = (x_1, x_2, \ldots, x_n) \qquad \mathbf{p}_i = (p_{i1}, p_{i2}, \ldots, p_{in})$

$\alpha_i = (\alpha_{i1}, \alpha_{i2}, \ldots, \alpha_{in}), \qquad m = 4, \qquad n = 3$

The region of interest is $0 \leqslant x_i \leqslant 1$.

i	α_i			c_i	p_i		
1	3.0	10.0	30.0	1.0	0.3689	0.117	0.2673
2	0.1	10.0	35.0	1.2	0.4699	0.4387	0.747
3	3.0	10.0	30.0	3.0	0.1091	0.8732	0.5547
4	0.1	10.0	35.0	3.2	0.03815	0.5743	0.8828

(5) *Shekel*

$$f(\mathbf{x}) = -\sum_{i=1}^{m} 1/[(\mathbf{x} - \mathbf{a}_i)^{\mathrm{T}} \cdot (\mathbf{x} - \mathbf{a}_i) + \mathbf{c}_i]$$

$\mathbf{x} = (x_1, x_2, \ldots, x_n)^{\mathrm{T}} \qquad \mathbf{a}_i = (x_{i1}, x_{i2}, \ldots, x_{in})^{\mathrm{T}}$

$\mathbf{c}_i > 0, n = 4, m = 5, 7, 10$

The region of interest is $0 \leqslant x_j \leqslant 10, j = 1, n$.

i	$\mathbf{a}_i$				$\mathbf{c}_i$
1	4	4	4	4	0.1
2	1	1	1	1	0.2
3	8	8	8	8	0.2
4	6	6	6	6	0.4
5	3	7	3	7	0.4
6	2	9	2	9	0.6
7	5	5	3	3	0.3
8	8	1	8	1	0.7
9	6	2	6	2	0.5
10	7	3.6	7	3.6	0.5

(6) *Shubert*

$$f(\mathbf{x}) = \left\{ \sum_{i=1}^{5} i \cos[(i+1)x_1 + i] \right\} \left\{ \sum_{i=1}^{5} i \cos[(i+1)x_2 + i] \right\}$$

The region of interest is $-10 \leqslant x_1, x_2 \leqslant 10$.

Appendix 2

In this appendix we shall list the DAP's built-in functions.

ALL	Takes a single logical vector or matrix argument and returns the logical AND of all components of the argument.
ALT	Takes a single-integer scalar argument of 32 bits and returns a logical vector. If the value of the argument modulo 62 is i, the logical vector will have its first i components FALSE, the next i components TRUE and so on in alternation. If $i = 0$, the result vector is FALSE.
ALTC	This is the same as ALT except that the result is a logical matrix, with alternating columns.
ALTR	This is the same as ALT except that the result is a logical matrix, with alternating rows.
ANDCOLS	Takes a logical matrix argument and returns a logical vector, each of whose values is the logical AND of the corresponding row or the argument.
ANDROWS	Same as ANDCOLS except the logical AND of the corresponding columns of the argument.
ANY	Takes a logical vector or matrix as an argument and returns with the logical OR of the argument.
COL	Takes an integer scalar or vector. If the argument is a scalar, then function returns with a logical matrix FALSE everywhere except for column i (which will be TRUE). If the argument is an integer vector, then the function returns with entry (i, j) = TRUE if the i component of the vector has the value j. If i is not within 1, 64, then all results are FALSE.
COLN	Takes a logical matrix and returns with an integer vector, each component of which is the index of the lowest column number in the corresponding row of the argument matrix which has the value TRUE. If a row is all FALSE, then the corresponding vector value is 0.

COLS — Takes two integer scalar arguments and returns with a logical matrix. If the arguments are *i* and *j*, then values in columns from *i* to *j* inclusive (of the resultant matrix) are set to TRUE. All other values are false; this also applies if either *i* or *j* are outside the range 1, 64.

EL — Takes a single integer scalar argument and returns with a logical vector. If the argument is *i*, then the *i* component of the vector is set to TRUE. All others are FALSE; they are also FALSE if *i* is not in the range 1, 64.

ELL — Same as EL except that it returns a logical matrix as its result and treats it as a long vector of 4096 values.

ELN — Takes a logical vector or matrix as an argument and returns with an integer scalar which indicates the position of the first TRUE component of the argument; again a matrix is treated as a long vector of 4096.

ELS — Takes two integer scalars as arguments and returns a logical vector. If the arguments are *i* and *j*, then values from *i* to *j* inclusive of the resultant vector are set to TRUE. All others are FALSE. If *I* or *j* are outside the range 1, 64, then all values are FALSE.

ELSL — Same as ELS except that it returns with a logical matrix with values from *i* to *j* set to TRUE. (Again the matrix is treated as a long vector of 4096.)

FRST — Takes a logical vector or matrix argument and returns with a logical value of the same mode with all values FALSE except for the position of the first TRUE value which is set to TRUE. If no component of the argument is TRUE, then no component of the result is TRUE.

LMATC — Takes a single scalar argument of any type and returns a logical matrix. The matrix result consists of 64 identical columns; the *i* component is TRUE iff the *i* but in the internal representation of the scalar argument is 1.

LMATR — Same as LMATC except that it returns with 64 identical rows.

MAT — Takes a single scalar argument of any type and returns a matrix value of the same type. Each component of the result is equal to the scalar argument.

MATC — Same as MAT except that it takes a vector argument

	and returns with a matrix with each column equal to the vector argument.
MATR	Same as MATC except that it returns with the rows equal to the vector argument.
MAXP	Takes two arguments: the first is a real or integer vector or matrix, and the second which is *optional* is a logical of the same mode as the first argument. The function returns with a logical of the same mode of the first which indicates via a TRUE value the position(s) of the maximum maxima in the first argument. The second argument can be used as a mask (that is search only for a maximum where the value of the second argument is TRUE).
MAXV	Same as for MAXP except that it returns with the numerical value of the maximum. The result is a scalar of the same type as the first operand.
MERGE	Takes three arguments of the same mode and returns a vector or matrix of the same type as the first and second arguments, the components of which are selected from either the first or the second argument depending on whether a TRUE or a FALSE value is in the third argument respectively.
MINP	Same as MAXP except that we indicate the position of the minimum.
MINV	Same as MAXV except that we return with the minimum value.
ORCOLS	Takes a single logical matrix and returns a logical vector, each component of which is the logical OR of all components in the corresponding row of the first argument.
ORROWS	Same as ORCOLS except that the logical OR of the columns is taken.
REV	Takes a single vector or matrix as an argument and reverses the order of the components (a matrix is treated as a long vector).
REVC	Takes a single matrix of any type and returns a matrix of the same type. The result consists of the argument with its column ordering reversed.
REVR	Same as REVC except for reordering of the rows.
ROW	Takes a single integer scalar or vector. If the argument is a scalar, then the result is a logical matrix set to FALSE except for row *i* which will be TRUE. If the argument is a vector, then the result is such that

$M(i, j) = \text{TRUE}$

if and only if the j component of the vector has the value i. If the integer scalar is not within 1, 64, then the entire resultant matrix is set to FALSE. If a component of a vector is not within 1, 64, then every component of the corresponding column of the logical matrix will be FALSE.

ROWN — Takes a single logical matrix argument and returns an integer vector, each component of which has the lowest row number in the corresponding column of the argument having the value TRUE. If all entries in a column are FALSE, the corresponding vector entry will be 0.

ROWS — Takes two integer scalar arguments and returns a logical matrix. If the values of the arguments are i and j, the components in rows from i to j inclusive of the result are set to TRUE. All others are FALSE. If i or j are not within 1, 64, then all values of the result are FALSE.

SHEC — Takes two arguments: the first is a matrix of any type, and the second (optional) an integer scalar. The value returned is a matrix the same type as argument 1, which has been shifted a number of places to the east, using cyclic geometry. The second argument determines the number of places of the shift (a default of 1 is assumed). If the second argument is an integer vector, each row of the resulting matrix is shifted by the number of places specified in the corresponding entry of the vector.

SHEP — Same as SHEC except that we use plane geometry.

SHLC — Takes two arguments: the first is a vector or matrix, and the second a scalar. The function returns a result of the same mode as the first argument shifted a number of places to the left (determined by the second argument). A matrix is treated as a long vector.

SHLP — Same as SHLC except that we use plane geometry.

SHNC — Same as SHEC except that the matrix is shifted to the north.

SHNP — Same as SHNC except that we use plane geometry.

SHRC — Same as SHLC except that we shift to the right.

SHRP — Same as SHRC except that we use plane geometry.

SHSC — Same as SHEC except that the matrix is shifted to the south.

SHSP	Same as SHSC except that we use plane geometry.
SHWC	Same as SHEC except that we shift to the west.
SHWP	Same as SHWC except that we use plane geometry.
SUM	Takes a vector or matrix as an argument and returns the sum of all components. If the argument is a logical type then TRUE is treated as 1 and FALSE as 0, and the result is of type integer.
SUMC	Takes a matrix of any type as an argument and returns a vector. The values in this vector are the sums of all values in the corresponding row of the matrix.
SUMR	Same as SUMC except that we sum the values in the columns.
TRAN	Takes a matrix and returns the transpose.
VEC	Takes a scalar argument and returns a vector. Each element of the vector is equal to the scalar argument.

Appendix 3

In this appendix, details of the implementations on the DAP will be given. First the formation of the gradient vector **g** and the product $\mathbf{p}^{\mathrm{T}} \cdot A\mathbf{p}$ as described in section 4.6 will be described in greater detail. Then the modifications necessary when there are three unknowns per node as in Chapter 5 will be detailed, and finally a description of how our diagonal scaling is achieved will be given.

First let us restate a few facts. Our local element and node numbering is given in Figs A3.1 and A3.2 respectively; note that all the element information is stored on the uppermost left processor.

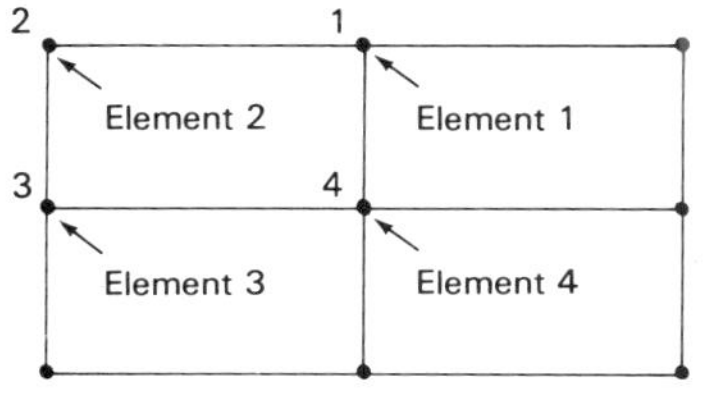

Fig. A3.1

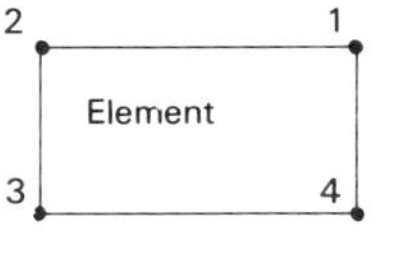

Fig. A3.2

The algorithm requires the formation of

$$g = \sum_{\mathrm{el}=1}^{4} g_{L(i)}^{\mathrm{el}}$$

where $L(i)$ converts the global node i into a local node for element el. On the assumption that for each element the equation (equation (4.10)) has been evaluated, then four values per element are stored

$$g_k^{\mathrm{el}} = \iint_{\mathrm{el}} \left[2K_x \frac{\partial \phi_k}{\partial x} \left(\sum \frac{\partial \phi_j}{\partial x} T_j \right) + 2K_y \frac{\partial \phi_k}{\partial y} \left(\sum \frac{\partial \phi_j}{\partial y} T_j \right) \right] \mathrm{d}V - 2Q_k$$

in an array GEL(,,4). As was mentioned in section 4.6, to form g at node * the function $L(i)$ will take the third value of g^{el} from element 1 plus the fourth value of g^{el} from element 2 plus the first value of g^{el} from element 3 plus the second value of g^{el} from element 4. When centred on node * then the third value from element 1 which comes from point 1 will be obtained by the expression GEL(−,,3) (this means select the third matrix of the set and shift it one place to the south), the fourth value from element 2 (point 2) will be obtained by GEL(−,−4), the first from element 3 (point 3) requires GEL(,−,1) and finally the second value from element 4 (point 4) is our current position GEL(,,2). The code therefore becomes

```
G=0
G(MASK1)=GEL(−,,3)+GEL(−,−,4)+GEL(,−,1)+GEL(,,2)
```

The MASK1 will take care of the region of interest (if less than 64 × 64 or a non-square region). The important point to note is that the above expression calculates *all values of vector* **g** *at once.* The product $\mathbf{g}^{\mathrm{T}} \cdot \mathbf{g}$ can now easily be worked out as follows:

```
GTG=SUM(G**2)
```

The second product required is $\mathbf{p}^{\mathrm{T}} \cdot A\mathbf{p}$. This time, instead of being centred at a particular node, the code is centred on an element; for example consider Fig. A3.3, where there is a 4 × 4 element matrix and four local values for P. Now P_1 will come from a shift of the form $P(,+)$, P_2 is our current position P, P_3 will come from a shift of P(+,), and P_4 will come from a shift of P(+,+). The produce will be evaluated in two stages: the first stage is

$$r_i^{\mathrm{el}} = \sum_{j=1}^{4} A_{ij}^{\mathrm{el}} p_j^{\mathrm{el}} \qquad \text{for } i = 1, 4$$

and the second

$$\mathbf{p}^{\mathrm{T}} \cdot A\mathbf{p} = \sum_{i=1}^{N} p_i r_i$$

where N is the number of grid points. Taking the first product, we shall assign each of the four P_i values into another matrix to facilitate a simplified (generalised) code; then a straightforward

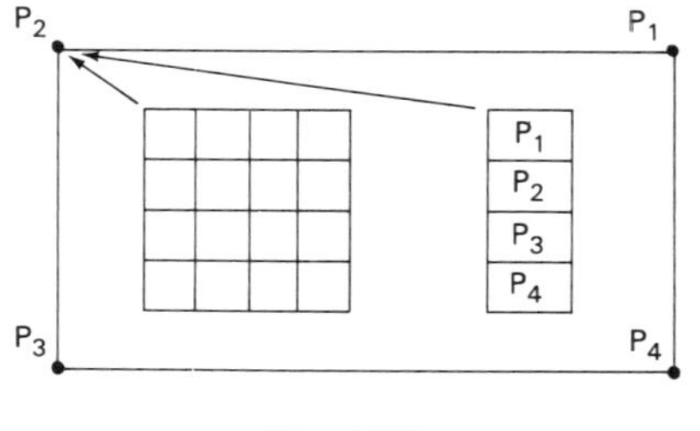

Fig. A3.3

matrix and vector product is performed between the 4 × 4 element matrix and the 4 × 1 local vector **P** shown in Fig. 3 The element matrix was obtained from the expression (equation (4.11))

$$\nabla^2 F_{ij} = \iint_{\text{el}} \left(2K_x \frac{\partial \phi_i}{\partial x} \frac{\partial \phi_j}{\partial x} + 2K_x \frac{\partial \phi_i}{\partial y} \frac{\partial \phi_j}{\partial y}\right) \mathrm{d}V$$

and has been stored in an array G2(,,4,4).

```
      CP(,,1)=P(,+)
      CP(,,2)=P
      CP(,,3)=P(+,)
      CP(,,4)=P(+,+)
      DO 5 I=1,4
 5      W(,,I)=0.0
      DO 10 I=1,4
      DO 10 I=1,4
 10     W(,,I)=W(,,I)+G2(,,I,J)*CP(,,J)
```

Having now performed this, each r is formed from the given information in W; this requires exactly the same operation as was required to form **g** at each node, that is

```
R=W(−,,3)+W(−,−,4)+W(,−,1)+W(,,2)
```

The second stage is simply

```
PTAP=SUM(P*R)
```

Some of the implementations needed in Chapter 5 will now be detailed.

The first point to be considered is what happens to the forming of the vector **g** when there are three unknowns per node; before this, however, let us examine how the 12 values (three unknowns and four nodes) are calculated for each of the elements using formulation I, for example.

Using equation (5) we have

$$g = 2 \sum \iint \left(w_1 e_1 \frac{\partial e_1}{\partial \mathbf{z}_j} + w_2 e_2 \frac{\partial e_2}{\partial \mathbf{z}_j} + w_3 e_3 \frac{\partial e_3}{\partial \mathbf{z}_j}\right) \mathrm{d}V$$

This gave equations (5.6a)–(5.6c) which can briefly be summarized as follows:

$$\text{unknown } 1 = -e_1 w_1 R \phi_i \sum b_k \phi_k - e_2 w_2 \frac{\partial \phi_i}{\partial x_1} - e_3 w_3 \frac{\partial \phi_i}{\partial x_2}$$

$$\text{unknown } 2 = e_1 w_1 \frac{\partial \phi_i}{\partial x_1} - e_1 w_1 R \phi_i \sum a_k \phi_k + e_2 w_2 \phi_i$$

$$\text{unknown } 3 = e_1 w_1 \frac{\partial \phi_i}{\partial x_2} + e_3 w_3 \phi_i$$

Let us now make the following assumptions.

(1) The same shifts are used as in Fig. A3.3.
(2) $\partial\phi_i/\partial x_i$, $\partial\phi_i/\partial x_2$, ϕ_i and w_i are readily available in PDX(,,4), PDT(,,4), SN(4) and WT(4) respectively.
(3) U(,,3) contains the unknowns as follows:U(,,1) all the a_i values; U(,,2) all the b_i values; U(,,3) all the c_i values.

The calculations can now be performed as follows:

(a) For $\sum a_i\phi_i$, $\sum b_i\phi_i$ and $\sum c_i\phi_i$

```
ASN=U(,+,1)*SN(1)+U(,,1)*SN(2)
     +U(+,,1)*SN(3)+U(+,+,1)*SN(4)

BSN=U(,+,2)*SN(1)+U(,,2)*SN(2)
     +U(+,,2)*SN(3)+U(+,+,2)*SN(4)

CSN=U(,+,3)*SN(1)+U(,,3)*SN(2)
     +U(+,,3)*SN(3)+U(+,+,3)*SN(4)
```

(b) For e_1, e_2 and e_3 as defined by equation (5.3a)–(5.3c)

```
E1=PDX(,,1)*U(,+,2)+PDY(,,1)*U(,+,3)
  +PDX(,,2)*U(,,2)+PDY(,,2)*U(,,3)
  +PDX(,,3)*U(+,,2)+PDY(,,3)*U(+,,3)
  +PDX(,,4)*U(+,+,2)+PDY(,,4)*U(+,+,3)
  -REN*ASN*BSN

E2=BSN-PDX(,,1)*U(,+,1)-PDX(,,2)*U(,,1)
       -PDX(,,3)*U(+,,1)-PDX(,,4)*U(+,+,1)

E3=CSN-PDY(,,1)*U(,+,1)-PDY(,,2)*U(,,1)
       -PDY(,,3)*U(+,,1)-PDY(,,4)*U(+,+,1)
```

All the information necessary to calculate the 12 previously mentioned values is now available. Assume the array EGD(,,12) exists for storing them. The code becomes

```
      DO 100 I=1,4
       PLANE=2*(I-1)+I
C      plane will always point to the start of node i
C      now calculate unknown 1 for node i.
       EGD(,,PLANE)=-E1*REN*WT(1)*SN(1)*BSN
                    -E2*WT(2)*PDX(,,I)
                    -E3*WT(3)*PDY(,,I)
     *
C      calculate unknown 2 for node i.
       EGD(,,PLANE+1)=E1*WT(1)*PDX(,,I)
     *                -E1*WT(1)*REN*SN(I)*ASN
     *                +E2*WT(2)*SN(I)
```

```
C        calculate unknown 3 for node i.
         EGD(,,PLANE+2)=E1*WT(1)*PDY(,,I)
     *                 +E3*WT(3)*SN(I)
 100  CONTINUE
      DO 150 I=1,12
         GEL(,,I)=GEL(,,I)+EGD(,,I)*GMULT
 150  CONTINUE
```

where GMULT is an integration factor obtained by a 3×3 quadrature; hence the code above must be contained inside a loop which will obtain the appropriate shape function and calculate the integration factor and then a contribution for each of the nine quadrature points. There may be some redundancy in the above code but this has been left in to avoid complicating the example with additional loops and variables.

Now, to form the three values of **g** per node, the actual code remains the same; however, it is enclosed inside a loop for $i=1, 3$ (the number of unknowns). Figure A3.4 illustrates the problem where we now have 12 values for each element (three unknowns and four nodes) which were obtained from equations (5.6a)–(5.6c) or (5.13a)–(5.13c) depending upon which formulation we used.

The contributions to **g** at node 5 will come from the area of the

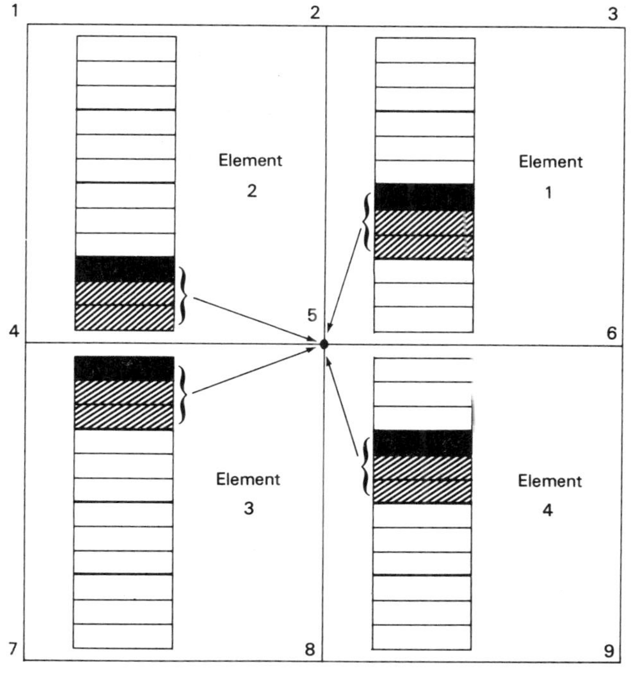

Fig. A3.4

element information which appears black in Fig. A3.4 and the code will become

```
G = 0
G(MASK1,1) = GEL(−,,7)+GEL(−,−,10)
             +GEL(,−,1)+GEL(,,4)
```

g at node 5 will come by

```
G(MASK1,2) = GEL(−,,8)+GEL(−,−,11)
             +GEL(,−,2)+GEL(,,5)
```

and **g** at node 5 by

```
G(MASK1,3) = GEL(−,,9)+GEL(−,−,12)
             +GEL(,−,3)+GEL(,,6)
```

which can, of course, be generalised to the following:

```
DO 100 I=1,3
G(MASK1,I)=GEL(−,,I+6)+GEL(−,−,I+9)
          +GEL(,−,I)+GEL(,,I+3)
100  CONTINUE
```

and the vector product $\mathbf{g}^T.\mathbf{g}$ now becomes

```
    GTG=0.0
    DO 150 I=1,3
150 GTG=GTG+SUM(G(,,I)**2)
```

The final calculation to be described is the diagonal scaling that was employed in section 5.6. Consider Fig. A3.5. Each element matrix is now 12×12 (three unknowns at each of four nodes) and this is stored with the uppermost left processor associated with that element In order to assemble the three values of a as given by

$$a_{ii} = \sum_{e=1}^{4} a^e_{L(i),\,L(i)}$$

for global node 5, only the (3 × 3) blocks indicated are used and in fact only the diagonals of those blocks are required. The code becomes.

```
   DO10I=1,3
   DIAG(MASK1,I)=G2(−,,I+6,I+6)×G2(−,−,I+9,I+9)+
                 G2(,−,I,I)+G2(,,I+3,I+3)
10 CONTINUE
```

Given this information the scaling described by equations (5.25)–(5.27) can now be undertaken.

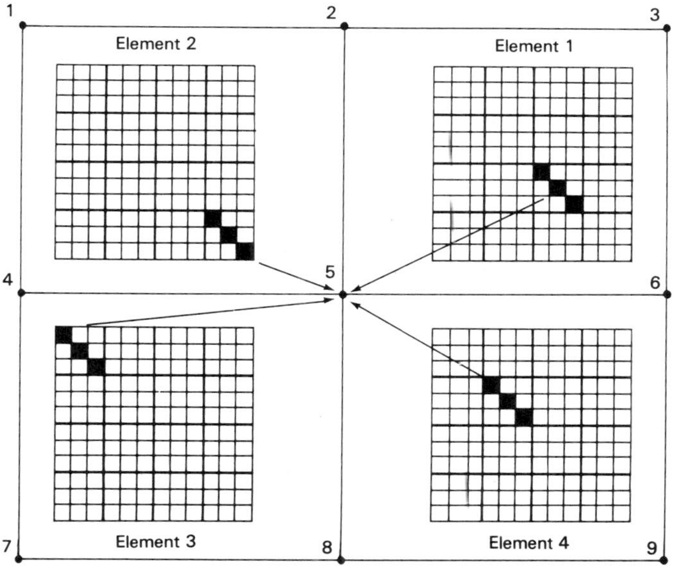

Fig. A3.5

The right-hand side vector **f** scaled by

$$\hat{f}_i = \frac{f_i}{\sqrt{a_{ii}}}$$

is simply

```
      DO 15 I=1,3
      F(MASK1,I)=F(,,I)/SORT(DIAG(,,I))
15    CONTINUE
```

Since the unknown vector **u** is initially zero, it requires no scaling, whilst the element matrices

$$\hat{a}_{ij} = \frac{a^e_{ij}}{\sqrt{(a_{G(i),G(i)}a_{G(j),G(j)})}}$$

require first the correct positioning of DIAG(,,I) in order for us to generalise the code

```
A(MASK1,1,1)=DIAG(,+,1)
A(MASK1,1,2)=DIAG(,+,2)
A(MASK1,1,3)=DIAG(,+,3)
A(MASK1,2,1)=DIAG(,,1)
A(MASK1,2,2)=DIAG(,,2)
A(MASK1,2,3)=DIAG(,,3)
```

```
A(MASK1,3,1)=DIAG(+,,1)
A(MASK1,3,2)=DIAG(+,,2)
A(MASK1,3,3)=DIAG(+,,3)
A(MASK1,4,1)=DIAG(+,+,1)
A(MASK1,4,2)=DIAG(+,+,2)
A(MASK1,4,3)=DIAG(+,+,3)
```

The scaling can now be expressed as

```
   DO 20 K=1,4
     ISI=3*(K-1)
     DO 20 L=1,4
       JS1=3*(L-1)
       DO 20 I=1,3
         IS = IS1+I
         DO 20 J=1,3
           JS = JS1+J
           G2(MASK,IS,JS)=G2(,,IS,JS)/SQRT(A(,,K,I)*A(,,LJ))
20 CONTINUE
```

On completion of the linear solver the solution must be rescaled to get back the solution of the original problem. Only the solution vector **u** needs to be rescaled (as the element matrices will be updated on the next iteration, and the right-hand side vector was preserved on entry) such that

$$u_i = \frac{u_i}{\sqrt{a_{ii}}}$$

the code being

```
     DO 30 I=1,3
       U(MASK1,I)=U(,,I)/SQRT(DIAG(,,I))
30   CONTINUE
```

The difference between MASK and MASK1 is that MASK masks off the unwanted elements, while MASK1 masks off the unwanted nodes.

There are several ways in which the above code could be speeded up slightly. Firstly we could have declared A(,,12) instead of A(,,4,3), which would save some indexing. Secondly, the square root of DIAG could have been taken before assigning it into A, thus saving 144 square roots which are required in the above loop for generating the correct G_2.

Appendix 4

A4.1 INTERPOLATION

Using Fig. A4.1, an expression for u can be defined as

$$u = u_1(1-x)(1-y) + u_2x(1-y) + u_3y(1-x) + u_4xy$$

and at the points $(\frac{1}{2}, 0)$ $(0, \frac{1}{2})$ and $(\frac{1}{2}, \frac{1}{2})$ the following are defined:

$$u = \tfrac{1}{2}u_1 + \tfrac{1}{2}u_2$$
$$u = \tfrac{1}{2}u_1 + \tfrac{1}{2}u_3$$

and

$$u = \tfrac{1}{2}(u_1 + u_2 + u_3 + u_4)$$

Then an expression u_5 at node * can be derived respectively

$$\begin{aligned} u_s &= u_1(1-2x)(1-2y) + (\tfrac{1}{2}u_1 + \tfrac{1}{2}u_2)2x(1-2y) \\ &\quad + (\tfrac{1}{2}u_1 + \tfrac{1}{2}u_3)2y(1-2x) \\ &\quad + \tfrac{1}{4}(u_1 + u_2 + u_3 + u_4)2x\,2y \\ &= u_1(1 - 2x - 2y + 4xy + x - 2xy + y - 2xy + xy) \\ &\quad + u_2(x - 2xy + xy) + u_3(y - 2xy + xy) + u_4xy \\ &= u_1(1 - x - y + xy) + u_2(x - xy) + u_3(y - xy) \\ &\quad + u_4xy \\ &= u \end{aligned}$$

and

$$\begin{aligned} \frac{\partial u_s}{\partial x} &= -u_1(1-y) + u_2(1-y) - u_3y + u_4y \\ &= \frac{\partial u}{\partial x} \end{aligned}$$

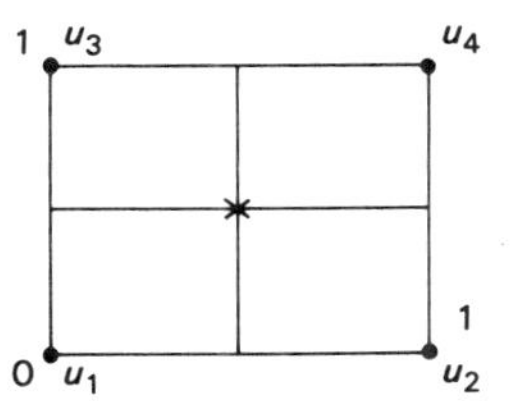

Fig. A4.1

Therefore, if the interpolation is performed correctly, all variables will remain the same at every point and hence the function value I will remain unaltered.

A4.2 SINGULARITIES

Consider Fig. A4.2 with a singularity at the corner. Then the contribution from

$$I = \int_0^h\!\!\int_0^h \mathbf{e}^{\mathrm{T}}\cdot\mathbf{e} \qquad \mathrm{d}A \to 1 + \frac{2u_2^2}{3} - u_2 \text{ as } h \to 0$$

Using the set of equations (7.6), it can be seen that the equations involving the singularity are e_1, e_2, e_4 and e_5. Writing out the singular part of each of these equations gives

$$e_1 = uu_x$$

$$e_2 = uv_x$$

$$e_4 = \frac{\partial u}{\partial x}$$

$$e_5 = \frac{\partial u}{\partial y}$$

Now by using the definition given in Fig. A4.1 the set (A4.1) can be expressed as

$$e_1^2 = \left[\left(u_1\left(1-\frac{x}{h}\right)\left(1-\frac{y}{h}\right) + u_2\frac{x}{h}\left(1-\frac{y}{h}\right) + u_3\frac{y}{h}\left(1-\frac{x}{h}\right) + u_4\frac{x}{h}\frac{y}{h}\right)\left(u_{x1}\left(1-\frac{x}{h}\right)\left(1-\frac{y}{h}\right) + u_{x1}\frac{x}{h}\left(1-\frac{y}{h}\right) + u_{x3}\frac{y}{h}\left(1-\frac{x}{h}\right) + u_{x4}\frac{x}{h}\frac{y}{h}\right)\right]^2$$

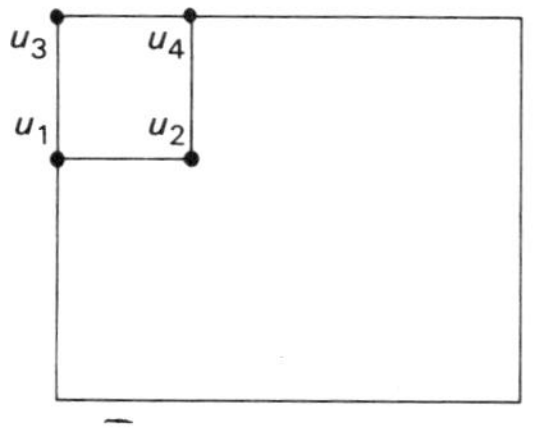

Fig. A4.2

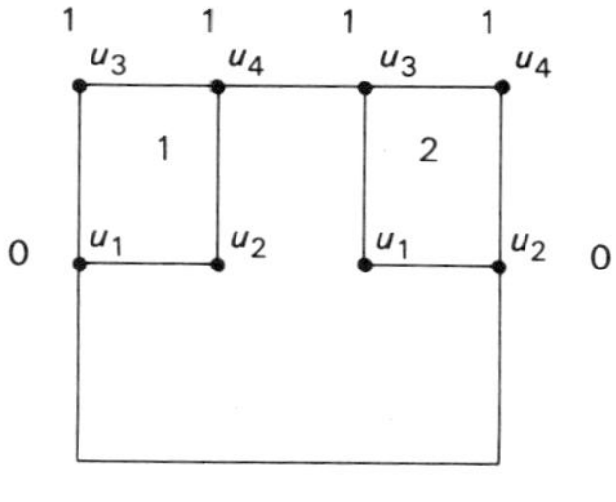

Fig. A4.3

$$= \left[\left(u_2 \frac{x}{h}\left(1 - \frac{y}{h}\right) + \frac{y}{h}\right)\left(u_{x1}\left(1 - \frac{x}{h}\right)\left(1 - \frac{y}{h}\right)\right.\right.$$

$$\left.\left. + u_{x2}\frac{x}{h}\left(1 - \frac{y}{h}\right) + u_{x3}\frac{y}{h}\left(1 - \frac{x}{h}\right) + u_{x4}\frac{x}{h}\frac{y}{h}\right)\right]^2$$

$$e_2^2 = \left[\left(u_2 \frac{x}{h}\left(1 - \frac{y}{h}\right) + \frac{y}{h}\right)\left(v_{x1}\left(1 - \frac{x}{h}\right)\left(1 - \frac{y}{h}\right)\right.\right.$$

$$\left.\left. + v_{x2}\frac{x}{h}\left(1 - \frac{y}{h}\right) + v_{x3}\frac{y}{h}\left(1 - \frac{x}{h}\right) + v_{x4}\frac{x}{h}\frac{y}{h}\right)\right]^2$$

$$e_4^2 = \left[\cancelto{0}{-\frac{u_1}{h}\left(1 - \frac{y}{h}\right)} + \frac{u_2}{h}\left(1 - \frac{y}{h}\right) - \frac{u_3}{h}\frac{y}{h} + \frac{u_4}{h}\frac{y}{h}\right]^2$$

$$= \left[\frac{u_2}{h}\left(1 - \frac{y}{h}\right)\right]^2$$

$$e_5^2 = \left[\cancelto{0}{-\frac{u_1}{h}\left(1 - \frac{x}{h}\right)} - \frac{u_2}{h}\frac{x}{h} + \frac{u_3}{h}\left(1 - \frac{x}{h}\right) + \frac{u_4}{h}\frac{x}{h}\right]^2$$

$$= \left[\frac{1}{h} - \frac{u_2}{h}\frac{x}{h}\right]$$

The integration over the element is

$$I_e = \int_0^h\!\!\int_0^h (e_5^2 + e_4^2 + e_2^2 + e_1^2)\,\mathrm{d}x\,\mathrm{d}y$$

$$= 1 + \frac{u_2^2}{3} - u_2 + u_2^2 + \frac{u_2^2}{3} - u_2^2 + O(h)$$

$$= 1 + \frac{2u_2^2}{3} - u_2 + O(h)$$

Therefore

$$I \to 2 + \frac{2u_2^2}{3} + \frac{2u_1^2}{3} - u_2 - u_1 + O(h)$$

the $2u_1^2/3$ term coming from the second singularity, namely element 2 in Fig. A4.3. As $h \to 0$, u_2 in element 1 will have a value in the range (0, 1) because of the interpolation; therefore the minimum value of I will occur when u_2 in element 1 and u_1 in element 22 both equal $\frac{3}{4}$ and the function value is $\frac{5}{4}$.

References

CHAPTER 1

[1] Fletcher, R., and Reeves, C. M., Function minimisation by conjugate gradients, *Computer Journal*, **7** (1964).
[2] Dixon, L. C. W., Non-linear Optimisation, Birkhauser, 1980, pp. 2–29.

CHAPTER 2

[1] Flynn, M., *IEEE Transactions on Computers*, **C-21**, 9 (1972), 948–960.
[2] Barlow, R. H., *et al.*, *A Guide to Using The Neptune Processing System*, Loughborough University of Technology.
[3] Johnson, D., *et al.*, *Automatic Partitioning of Programs in a Multiprocessor System.*, Texas Instruments, Austin, Texas, (1979).
[4] Sauber, W. (ed.), *A Dataflow Architecture Implementation*, Texas Instruments, Austin, Texas, (1980).
[5] da-Silva, J. G. D., and Woods, J. V., Design of a processing subsystem for the Manchester data-flow computer, *Proceedings of the IEEE*, **128**, 5 (1981).
[6] Super-computers 1, *State of the Art Report*, Infotech, (1979).
[7] Super-computers 2, *State of the Art Report*, Infotech, (1979).
[8] Reddaway, S. F., *The DAP Approach*, ICL, Stevenage, (1979).
[9] Flanders, P. M., *FORTRAN Extensions for a Highly Parallel Processor*, ICL, Stevenage, (1979).
[10] DAP: introduction to FORTRAN programming, *Technical Publication 6755*, ICL, Stevenage, (1978).
[11] DAP: FORTRAN language, *Technical Publication 6918*, ICL, Stevenage, (1981).
[12] DAP developing DAP programs, *Technical Publication 6920*, ICL, Stevenage, (1981).
[13] Singh, P., An investigation into the prediction of the flow of viscous incompressible fluids, Ph.D. Thesis, The Hatfield Polytechnic, 1983.

CHAPTER 4

[1] Hestenes, M. and Stiefel, E., Methods of conjugate gradients for solving linear systems, *Journal of the National Bureau of Standards*, **49**, (1952).
[2] Fletcher, R., and Reeves, C. M., Function minimisation by conjugate gradients, *Computer Journal*, **7**, (1964).
[3] Dixon, L. C. W., *Non-linear Optimisation*, English Universities Press, (1973).
[4] Stone, N. L., Iterative solution of implicit approximations of multi-dimensional partial differential equations, *SIAM Journal on Numerical Analysis*, **5**, 3 (1968).

CHAPTER 5

[1] Fletcher, R., and Reeves, C. M., Function minimisation by conjugate gradients. *Computer Journal*, **7**, (1964).
[2] Armijo, L. *Pacific Journal of Mathematics*, **16** 1966, 1–16.
[3] Forsythe, G., and Moler, C. B., *Computer Solution of Linear Algebraic Systems*, Prentice-Hall, 1967.
[4] Kightley, J. R., and Jones, I. P., A note on the vectorisation of preconditioned conjugate gradient algorithms, *Proceedings of the Second International Conference on Vector and Parallel Processors in Computational Science, Oxford, August 1984*, in press.

CHAPTER 7

[1] Singh, P., An investigation into the prediction of the flow of viscous incompressible fluids, *Ph D. Thesis*, The Hatfield Polytechnic, (1983).

CHAPTER 8

[1] *Proceedings of the Second International Conference on Vector and Parallel Processors in Computational Science, Oxford, August 1984*, in press.
[2] Simpson, P., and Merrifield, B. C., *Proceedings of the Second International Conference on Vector and Parallel Processors in Computational Science, Oxford, August 1984*, in press, pp. 133–140.
[3] Wait, R., and Martindale, I., Iterative solution of the three-dimensional finite elements on the DAP, *Proceedings of the Second International Conference on Vector and Parallel Processors in Computational Science, Oxford, August 1984*, in press.

APPENDIX 1

[1] Dixon, L. C. W., and Szego, G. P. (eds), *Towards Global Optimisation 2*, North-Holland, (1978).
[2] Price, W. L., A heuristic CRS algorithm, in Dixon, L. C. W., and Szego, G. P. (eds), *Towards Global Optimisation 2*, North-Holland, (1978).
[3] Price, W. L., A new version of the controlled random search procedure for global optimisation, *Technical Report*, Engineering Department, University of Leicester, (1981).
[4] Dixon, L. C. W., and Patel, K. D., The place of parallel computation in numerical optimisation, II, the multi-extremal optimisation problem, *Technical Report 119*, Numerical Optimisation Centre, The Hatfield Polytechnic, (1981).

Index